Passport to Learn

Passport to Learn

Projects to Challenge High-Potential Learners

Jacque Melin

Zephyr Press

Tucson, Arizona

Passport to Learn: Projects to Challenge High-Potential Learners

Grades 4–8

©2001 by Jacque Melin

Printed in the United States of America

ISBN 1-56976-125-6

Editor: Bonnie Lewis
Design & Production: Dan Miedaner
Illustrations: Margie and Chris Smallfield
Cover: Dan Miedaner

Published by:
Zephyr Press
P.O. Box 66006
Tucson, Arizona 85728-6006
800-232-2187
www.zephyrpress.com
www.giftsforteachers.com

Library of Congress Cataloging-in-Publication Data

Melin, Jacque, 1945-
    Passport to learn : projects to challenge high-potential learners / Jacque Melin.
        p. cm.
    Includes bibliographical references
    ISBN 1-56976-125-6 (alk. paper)
    1. Gifted children—Education—United States—Curricula. 2. Special education—Activity
    programs—United States. I. Title.

LC3993.9 .M45 2001
    371.95'6—dc21   00-043885

Acknowledgments
Thank You! Thank You! Thank You! Thank You! Thank You!

To Maggie and John

. . . for your loving support and faith in me, and for letting me hog the computer during these months.

Throughout my life, I have been supported by people who have helped me expand my horizons. I have worked with many gifted educators, who introduced me to some of the ideas in this book or have collaborated with me to develop challenging curriculum materials. Martha Kaufeldt, Zephyr Press author of *Begin with the Brain* and a longtime friend and associate, was the first to challenge me to take on this project after I retired from public education.

During my 32 happy years with Rockford Public Schools, there are dozens of colleagues to whom I owe abundant thanks. Special thanks to Mike Micele, assistant superintendent for instruction, who believed it was important to help our enthusiastic staff plan worthwhile projects and activities for the gifted children in our district. Mike supported a variety of initiatives for our teachers. These included developing brain-compatible integrated thematic units; training new staff to use higher-level thinking skills through the Dimensions of Learning model; and supporting talent workshops where our own teachers shared challenging ideas, strategies, and activities.

During the talent workshops, several staff members developed and field-tested some of the activities included in this book. The following teachers deserve special recognition as ticket authors: Mary Ellen Thienes developed "What's Up When You're Down?"; Sonia Andrews, Linda Critchell, Nancy McPhee, and Ann Wilson designed "Been There—Done That"; Lisa DeWitt and Linda Warren collaborated to produce "WWYD: What Would You Do?"

Dear friends, Gail Falcinelli and Joan Dreyer, must be thanked for their ever-helpful suggestions and contributions in "More on Oxymoron," "Seven Up, Joust Do It," and "Thrill Seekers." Gail's clever family also helped to develop the interesting titles for the activities in this book. Thank you Jim, Laura, and Lisa.

I am forever grateful to my illustrators and graphic artists: former student Chris Smallfield and his mother, Margie Smallfield. They came up with a fresh illustration each time I had a new idea. Their artwork makes me very proud of this book. This is the first book they have illustrated together.

I am appreciative of the following educators and friends for their encouragement, support, and experience that helped enrich *Passport to Learn*: Dr. Dorothy Armstrong, Mary Nell Baldwin, Dr. Sherry Collins, Lori Finnerty, Wendy Carlson, Kim Fowle, Sue Kalee, Susan Kovalik, Susan Laninga, Alison Libby, Melissa Pischner-Stull, Kathleen and Dickson Small, and Sharon Wells.

Rockford Public School students used or piloted all of the activities included in this book. Special thanks to the following ambitious and talented students: Lisa Arndt, Brittany Bronsink, Aaron Bruinsma, Samantha Chamberlain, Brittney Clark, Katie Esch, Elizabeth Fox, Scott Fults, Josh Gates, Emily Gremel, Lizzie Haworth-Hoeppnar, Elyse Welcher, and Clarke Wolf.

Finally, Jessica Knoll, one of my graduate students from Grand Valley State University, stuck with me from lofty ideas to subtle crashes as we edited the text before sending it off to Zephyr Press. Thank you Jessica! This quote is for you:

Great ideas need landing gear as well as wings.
—C.D. Jackson

Table of Contents

Preface

Oh, I have slipped the surly bonds of earth,
And danced the skies on laughter-silvered wings
. . . and done a hundred things you have not dreamed of . . .

—John Gillespie Magee, Jr., from "High Flight"

A Note from Your Captain

As a teenager, I would stay up until midnight just so I could watch the television station sign off for the day. (I know, I'm showing my age—TV stations don't even sign off anymore!) At midnight, our local station would play the "Star Spangled Banner." This was followed by a short film of a plane soaring through the clouds as the poem "High Flight" was read.

It was during those years that I thought about expanding my own horizons and wondered if I would ever achieve those hundreds of things of which I had dreamed...

The dream of becoming a pilot persisted in my thoughts when I started teaching. Consequently, I also took a part-time receptionist job at the airport so that I could earn the extra cash needed to take flying lessons. At age 25, I became a pilot—fulfilling a longtime goal.

I have been very fortunate to be able to continue to pursue hundreds of exciting experiences and goals—some that I had dreamed of, some not. I became a scuba diver, had a beautiful daughter, traveled to many parts of the world, taught various grade levels in school, became the gifted/talented coordinator for my district, served as an elementary principal, and retired. Now, lo and

behold, I am writing a book! That love of flying continues to be a part of me; hence the aviation theme for *Passport to Learn: Projects to Challenge High-Potential Learners.*

Passport to Learn is the result of 33 years of personal experience as an educator. I have always maintained a special focus upon creating lessons, designing curricula, and implementing programs that target the special needs of high-potential students. In order to simultaneously engage learners of all abilities in my classroom, I produced a variety of strategies and materials. Sometimes, I used the newly developed ideas with my entire class, because they were things that everyone would enjoy and that would enrich what we were studying. Often, I used the material with groups of students when I met with different ability levels for instructional purposes. Other times, I compacted the curriculum (especially during reading and math) for my gifted students, and gave them choices from the materials that could be done independently.

In order to keep my gifted students motivated to work independently and to make sure they were learning important thinking, organizational, and study skills, I devised a plan where students received a learning contract for independent studies in the form of a ticket aboard Expanding Horizons Airlines. Students were assessed on their independent projects on a frequent-flyer point system. When students completed their *Tickets for Success,* they earned *Frequent-Flyer Miles.* The goal was to receive enough frequent-flyer miles to make it around the world during the school year. Students enjoyed charting their miles on a world map and *Passport.* They also relished receiving *Passport Stamps* each time they reached one of the 12 destination cities on their trip around the world.

During this time, I was using different types of lessons and motivators with the rest of my class, so no one felt that these students were getting something "special" for their efforts. They were simply following a curriculum that was more appropriate for their skills and abilities. My gifted students often shared the results of their independent studies with the rest of the class. Other students sometimes were stimulated to attempt some of these additional challenges. That was fine with me. Even though I could not compact the curriculum for some of my students, they were always welcome to work on these projects if they desired.

All of the activities in *Passport to Learn* have been used successfully with high-potential students. I have compiled and published these strategies to help other teachers. At your fingertips are a variety of open-ended, challenging ideas to better meet the needs of these students. The enriching and meaningful activities may even inspire you to develop some of your own *Tickets for Success.* The management system suggested in this book can be tailored to fit your individual teaching style. Happy landings! ❦

Chapter 1
Preparing for Takeoff

As a committed, resourceful, but very busy educator, you would love to engage all of your students all of the time. Due to the lack of time and convenient materials, however, the goal of providing specialized, enriching, and challenging tasks for your high-potential students often takes the back burner to more immediate needs.

Educators regularly encounter gifted students who have mastered 30 to 50 percent of the grade-level curriculum before it has even been presented. Several of these high-achieving students may spend less than an hour of the day actually engaged in learning. When the proper stimulation for these sharp and agile young minds is not provided, we risk losing these promising students to boredom and apathy.

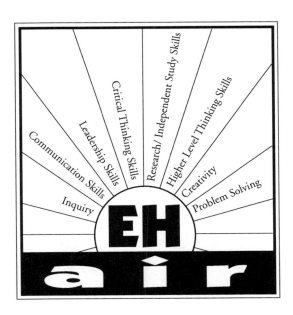

The Right Stuff

Gifted students possess potential for independent and critical thinking and benefit from active exploration, questioning, and investigation. As teachers, we can expand the horizons for these high-potential students by compacting their curriculum. Curriculum compacting is a procedure for modifying the grade-level curriculum for high-ability students by eliminating materials they have already mastered. We can then provide these students with an alternative learning program that is stimulating, challenging, and motivating.

The *Tickets for Success* in this book are independent-study projects that target and help develop the following skills:

- communication
- creative thinking
- critical thinking
- higher-level thinking
- inquiry
- leadership
- problem solving
- research and independent study

Passport to Learn: Projects to Challenge High-Potential Learners provides you with an entire program of ready-to-use activities that will help your gifted students take off. It is a compilation of high-flying adventures designed to open windows of opportunity and possibility, expanding the horizons for your high-potential upper elementary and middle school students.

Welcome Aboard Expanding Horizons Airlines

As their teacher and travel agent for Expanding Horizons Airlines, you will have some organizational and planning work to get your students started on the *Passport to Learn* program. However, once your world travelers are identified and provided with tools for their journey, the projects are designed to be student-directed, self-paced, and independent. Once the program is in place, your students take control of their own learning.

What's Included

**Teacher/Travel Agent Tools—
Deciding Who Is Ready to Travel**
- Who's at the Gate? (assessment tool)
- Interest Inventory
- Sample Letter to Parents
- Checking In: Goals Inventory
- Checking In at the Gate Goals
- Travel Agent's Deskplate (for your desk)
- Flight Attendants' Buttons (nametags for parent helpers)

**Making Travel Plans—
Preparing the Student Traveler**
- 5 Departure Screens
- Passport Application
- Ticket Jacket
- Passport
- Frequent-Flyer Miles Map
- Suitcase (organizer)

Necessities for the Student Traveler
- Flight Log (planner and evaluation tool)
- 50 Tickets for Success
- Boarding Passes
- 12 Destination City Passport Stamps
- Certificate of Completion

The Travel Plan

Determine which students in your class should participate in this program by using the *Who's at the Gate?* assessment tool (page 10) and administering the *Interest Inventory* (page 11). Decide what goals should be targeted for each student you select, using the *Checking In: Goals Inventory* (page 14).

Arrange to meet with each student and his or her parent(s) to discuss the program. A sample letter you can use is included on page 13. At this meeting, ask the student to complete a *Passport Application* (page 25) in order to make a reservation for this special undertaking. Together, with the student and parent(s), develop an individualized plan of action. Using the *Departure Screens* (pages 20–24) to gain an overview of the types of projects available, select the desired *Tickets for Success* (beginning on page 47). Note them down on *Checking In at the Gate Goals* (page 16). As the travel agent, you will completely fill out the front of a *Ticket Jacket* (see page 26), which will help the student keep track of his or her personal progress.

Once this plan is in place, present the first-time flyer with a folder, or *Suitcase* (page 28), in which to store his or her plans, research, and related materials. Additionally, the student will be given a *Passport* (page 31) for recording current and completed flights, frequent-flyer miles earned, *Stamps* (page 45) for destination cities that have been reached, personal information, and a photo. A *Frequent-Flyer Miles Map* (page 27) will help each student visually track his or her progress toward the eventual goal of traveling around the world.

Every time a student begins a new project, he or she should receive a new *Ticket for Success*. Each ticket outlines the details of the project and provides instructions in the form of an itinerary. Also, present the accompanying *Boarding Pass(es)*, which contain(s) supplemental information that will help the student complete the assignment. Finally, include a *Flight Log* (page 35), which contains checklists, focusing questions, log sheets, planning sheets, and other materials that will benefit the student on each project.

Once the student has looked over all of the project materials, he or she will submit to you a proposed plan of action on the *Charting Your Course* page (page 37), which is included in the *Flight Log*. From the point that you approve the plan, the project responsibilities lie solely with that high-potential learner. (Of course, students will have questions, and will be required to check in periodically with you throughout the project.)

Evaluation of the project will result from the combination of a student self-evaluation and your evaluation. A form for this purpose is provided in the *Flight Log* (page 44). *Frequent-Flyer Miles* earned (points for successful completion of elements on the form) can be recorded in the student's *Passport,* and distance can be mapped out on the student's map. When a student reaches or surpasses a destination city, provide that student with a *Stamp* (page 45) for his or her *Passport.*

Ultimately, the students participating in this program are working toward the goal of circumnavigating the globe. When a student accomplishes this goal, present a *Certificate of Completion* (page 46) for his or her hard work, discovery, and accomplishments.

Steps to Implementing *Passport to Learn*

Passport to Learn

Step 1: Understand the program.

Step 2: Decide who will participate.

Step 3: Determine the best direction for each student.

Step 4: Review expectations with the student and parent(s).

Step 5: Organize the traveler's materials.

Step 6: Takeoff!

Step 7: Check in to monitor progress.

Step 8: Evaluate, then book the next flight.

Step One: Understand the Program

Study this introduction, read through the various student projects, and review the various forms, materials, and resources provided in this book. Each project, or *Ticket to Success,* has a designated flight number. This number begins with EH (for Expanding Horizons Airlines) and contains other letters and numbers according to content area and project number. Content areas have been abbreviated as *LA* for Language Arts, *LS* for Leadership Studies, *M* for Mathematics, *SC* for Sciences, and *SS* for Social Studies. For example, the flight designated as *EH-LA1* is Expanding Horizons Airlines, Language Arts project number 1, and so on.

Step Two: Decide Who Will Participate

Who's at the Gate? "Behaviors"

Read the behaviors listed below. Write the names of the students in your class who exhibit these behaviors in the boxes under each listed behavior. A student's name may appear in more than one box. After you have completed this sheet, please give the *Interest Inventory* (page xx) to those students whose names you have listed here.

Composite scores on achievement tests and intelligence tests are very high	Scores high on specific areas of achievement tests
Learns rapidly, easily, and efficiently	Is an independent learner
Comprehends easily and/or has an extensive vocabulary	Is clear and accurate in oral and/or written expression
Demonstrates creative ideas	Understands abstract concepts
Demonstrates leadership abilities	Demonstrates superior musical, artistic, or technological skills

The *Who's at the Gate?* informal survey of behaviors (page 10) will help you target particular students whose learning potential might benefit from an enriched curriculum. Students may fit into more than one category. Write the students' names into the categories provided. After completing the page, study it carefully and ask yourself questions such as the following:

- Am I challenging the students who are listed on this page?
- Am I teaching these students things they already know?
- Can I compact the curriculum for all or some of these students, then have them do things that are more relevant for their ability levels?
- What are these students interested in doing?
- What skills should these students be developing?

Step Three: Determine the Best Direction for Each Student

Interest Inventory: Informally, you have surveyed your students to find those who need to be more challenged. This *Interest Inventory* (page 11) provides you with information about what would make learning more relevant for these students. Administer this inventory to all of the students in your class or just to those whose names appear on your *Who's at the Gate?* list. This inventory provides valuable information that can help you expand the horizons of your high-potential students throughout the school year.

Checking In at the Gate Goals: Set some goals for teaching these students the skills that you would like to see them learn during the school year. Photocopy one *Checking In at the Gate Goals* (page 16) checklist for each student whose curriculum you are considering for compacting.

> Compacting can most easily be done during your language-arts block and sometimes during your mathematics block. Most often, it is obvious which students have already mastered the lessons you are teaching to the rest of your class. Sometimes, however, you may have to pretest students so you are certain that they have mastered the curriculum.

This checklist is for your personal files, and should be referred to throughout the year as you work with the student and check in on his or her progress. Transfer only the skills that you are sure the student will be able to accomplish for a grading period, semester, or year to the *Checking in the Gate Goals* checklist.

Step Four: Review Expectations with the Student and Parent(s)

Formulate a Plan: Set an appointment to introduce the *Passport to Learn* program to the selected student and his or her parent(s). Use the *Sample Letter to Parent(s)* on page 13 to invite them or write your own. At the meeting, explain that you would like the student to have the opportunity to work on material that would be more relevant to his or her abilities. At the same time, projects will target specific skills (communication, creative thinking, critical thinking, higher-level thinking, inquiry, leadership, problem solving, and research and independent study) that will continue to be important throughout his or her academic, professional, and personal life.

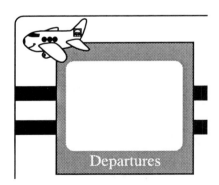

Departure Screens: Use the results from the *Interest Inventory*, the *Checking In: Goals Inventory* checklist, as well as the student's and parents' verbal input to pinpoint the type of enrichment projects that will be best for the learner. Look at the menu of optional projects offered on the *Departure Screens* (pages 20–24). Introduce a sample *Ticket for Success* (beginning on page 26) that you think the student would enjoy to help illustrate the program and its projects.

Inform the student and parent(s) that you will designate certain times of the day when the student may work on this *Ticket for Success*. Explain that the student will work alone on this project or, at times, may pair with another student. Point out also that other students may be working on different tickets during the designated times.

Ticket Jacket: Work together to select projects from the *Departure Screens* that will both challenge and interest the student. Designate the order in which each project is to be completed. Once these projects have been selected, copy those flight numbers onto the *Ticket Jacket* (page 26). The first project will be the *Flight of Origin*; the subsequent projects will be *Connecting Flights*. This jacket will remain in the possession of the student, who will use it as a long-term plan for project completion. However, the flight schedule can be updated or revised at any time to better accommodate a student's changing interests and needs.

Passport Application: In order to make a reservation for this exciting adventure, the student next will complete a *Passport Application* (page 25), in which he or she agrees to certain working conditions, to maintain a positive attitude, and to strive for a best effort. After filling out the application and discussing the working conditions with the student and parent(s), each of you should sign the application indicating that all parties agree to the conditions.

Passport: At this point, take an instant or digital camera picture of the student (or have the student draw a self-portrait), fill out a copy of the *Passport* (pages 30–33) together, assemble, and present it to the new traveler. Explain that the *Passport* is the record-keeping device to track *Frequent-Flyer Miles* (points) that are accumulated as the student completes *Tickets for Success*.

Stamps: All students begin their journey in San Francisco and go west around the world. This *Stamp* is glued or taped into the *Passport* in the indicated area. Each time he or she arrives at or passes a destination city, another *Stamp* (page 45) is earned for the *Passport*.

Frequent-Flyer Miles Map: Give each student a copy of the *Frequent-Flyer Miles Map* (page 27). Each time the student receives a final evaluation on a *Ticket for Success,* he or she should color in one dot for every 100 miles earned. Each student can easily track how far away he or she is from desired destinations, as well as the ultimate goal of circumnavigating the world.

Step Five: Organize the Traveler's Materials

Suitcase: The *Suitcase* graphic (page 28) can be affixed easily to a folder or some other carrying device for the *Tickets for Success, Passport, Boarding Passes, Ticket Jacket, Frequent-Flyer Miles Map, Flight Logs,* research resources, works in progress, and any other related materials.

A Note on the Internet

Many of the projects in this book ask the student to use the Internet as a research tool. It is advised that you discuss appropriate Internet use with each student. Some suggestions to share:

- Caution the student that the first site is not always the best source of information.

- Explain that knowing how to find and evaluate information through the Internet is a complex and important skill.

- Teach the student that using specific and precise keywords and protocol is essential if he or she is to work "smart" rather than work "hard." Acknowledge that it is common and frustrating to be led to sites that are no longer in operation or have moved.

- Finally, but most importantly, encourage the student always to ask critical questions of himself or herself while evaluating the quality and usefulness of a site. Some information is provided by reputable organizations and people who are well versed, present information fairly, and can be trusted. However, anyone can post information on the Internet. This means that many sites contain false information posted for questionable reasons by people who are uninformed or seek to misinform. Teach the student to always ascertain: Who provided this information? Why? Can this source be trusted? Are there any suspicious signs of a personal agenda or false information?

Make a copy of the completed *Ticket Jacket* from your meeting with the student and parent(s) for your files, then prepare all of the related materials for the student's takeoff. Make sure that you are able to provide any resources that the student will need before he or she begins.

Carefully read over each *Ticket for Success* and *Boarding Pass* that a student is ready to begin. Point out that each project requires different types and numbers of resources for successful completion. Some projects provide all of the necessary resources within the *Ticket* and *Boarding Pass*, some require specific resources, while others may be enhanced by resources but do not require them.

Flight Log: Give the student a new *Flight Log* (pages 35–44) for each new project. Photocopy the 10-page packet of information. Explain that the packet contains several tools that will help the student plan the project, record its progress, arrange useful checklists, and provide needed information. In particular, point out the *Charting Your Course* page (page 37) to the student. After he or she has looked over all of the flight materials, the student's first order of business will be to check in with you, armed with a plan, projected points for other proposed goals or benchmarks, and ETAs (estimated times of arrival, or estimated completion times). This *Charting Your Course* exercise alone will help the student develop strong task-analysis and time-management skills.

Tickets for Success and *Boarding Passes*: Photocopy the first *Ticket for Success* and corresponding *Boarding Pass(es)* (beginning on page 47) that your student has selected. Present these to the student. Each *Ticket for Success* features the itinerary (or plan) that the student should follow to

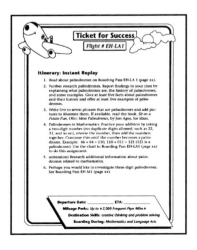

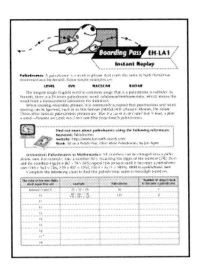

complete the ticket. Any changes to the itinerary should be approved by you. Additionally, each ticket includes a box in the lower right corner. Information in this box includes:

- *Departure date*: Record the date when the student begins this ticket.
- *ETA* (estimated time of arrival): Record the date when the student expects to complete this ticket.
- *Mileage perks*: This indicates the maximum number of *Frequent-Flyer Miles* that can be earned for that ticket. Most tickets are worth up to 2,000 *Frequent-Flyer Miles*. However, a few tickets are worth up to 4,000 or 6,000 *Frequent-Flyer Miles*, due to the level of difficulty or time that those tickets will require to complete.
- *Destination skills*: These are the target skills for the selected *Ticket for Success*. When you are conferencing with the student, emphasize the importance of developing these skills.
- *Boarding during*: This indicates the best time for a student to work on a ticket, which is after he or she has already mastered the curriculum that is being taught in the subject(s) stated.

Step Six: Take Off!

You are now ready to send the student off on the first leg of his or her journey around the world. Remind the student about the first proposed check-in, then let him or her take off!

Step Seven: Check In to Monitor Progress

A pattern for checking in with the student is established on the *Chart Your Course* planner in the *Flight Log*. In addition to the formal check-ins, ask to see the student's *Flight Log* and work-in-progress results as often as you see fit. In the beginning, you may wish to check in quite often— at least three times per week—to make sure the student is on the right course.

Step Eight: Evaluate Then Book the Next Flight

When a student has completed a project, use the evaluation instrument (page 44), provided within the *Flight Log* to award the appropriate number of *Frequent-Flyer Miles*. It is important that both the student and the teacher complete an evaluation and supply solid and meaningful justifications for the scores granted. This evaluation should include discussion and conversation, which is always more effective than merely recording a score on paper.

Now the high-potential student can record the miles earned within his or her *Passport*, as well as chart out the covered miles on the *Frequent-Flyer Miles Map*. If a student has reached or surpassed a destination city, he or she should also receive a *Passport Stamp*. The student is then ready to begin another ticket.

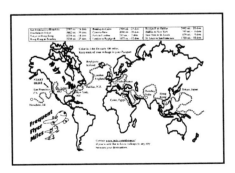

If and when a student successfully completes a trip around the world, a special *Certificate of Completion* (page 46) should be presented. ❧

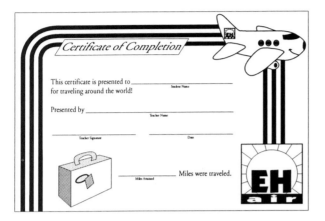

Preparing for First-Time Flyers

Photocopy the *Suitcase* cover (page 28) and glue it to a pocket or file folder for each participating student. Next, pack each student's *Suitcase*:

1. Photocopy the chosen *Tickets for Success*.

2. Photocopy the related *Boarding Passes*. Most (not all) tickets have a corresponding *boarding pass;* some *boarding passes* continue for several pages.

3. Photocopy, assemble, and staple a *Passport* (pages 31–33) for each student. See directions for assembling the *Passport* on page 30.

4. Photocopy, assemble, and staple a *Flight Log* (see pages 35–44) for each student. This 10-page booklet will be given to the student each time he or she begins a ticket.

5. Photocopy *Passport Stamps* and cut along broken lines (see page 45). Photocopy several pages of the *Passport Stamps* and cut them apart, making one labeled envelope for each destination city. Give a *Stamp* to a student each time he or she reaches a destination city.

6. Photocopy two *Ticket Jackets* (see page 26) per student: one for the student and one for you. The *Ticket Jacket* should be filled out during a conference with the student and parent(s).

7. Photocopy a *Frequent-Flyer Miles Map* for each student (see page 27).

8. Provide a list of scheduled check-in times for each student.

Chapter 2

Teacher/Travel Agent Tools

Deciding Who Is Ready to Travel

- Who's at the Gate?
- Interest Inventory
- Sample Letter to Parent(s)
- Checking In: Goals Inventory
- Checking In at the Gate Goals
- Travel Agent's Deskplate
- Flight Attendants' Buttons

"Aerodynamically, the bumblebee shouldn't be able to fly, but the bumble-bee doesn't know it so it goes on flying anyway."

—Mary Kay Ash

Who's at the Gate? "Behaviors"

Read the behaviors listed below. Write the names of the students in your class who exhibit these behaviors in the box under each listed behavior. A student's name may appear in more than one box. After you have completed this sheet, give the *Interest Inventory* (page 11) to the students whose names you have listed here.

Composite scores on achievement tests and intelligence tests are very high.	Scores high on specific areas of achievement tests.
Learns rapidly, easily, and efficiently.	Is an independent learner.
Comprehends easily and/or has an extensive vocabulary.	Is clear and accurate in oral and/or written expression.
Demonstrates creative ideas.	Understands abstract concepts.
Demonstrates leadership abilities.	Demonstrates superior musical, artistic, or technological skills.

1. Student name: _____

2. Grade: _____

3. Favorite school subject(s):

❑ Math   ❑ Spelling

❑ Reading   ❑ Art

❑ Writing   ❑ Music

❑ Science   ❑ Physical Education

❑ Social Studies

4. Least favorite school subject(s):

❑ Math   ❑ Spelling

❑ Reading   ❑ Art

❑ Writing   ❑ Music

❑ Science   ❑ Physical Education

❑ Social Studies

5. What are your hobbies, collections, or interests? _____

_____

_____

6. If you could travel anywhere in the world, where would you go? _____

_____

7. If you could spend a day with a famous person (living or deceased), who would that be?

_____

8. What is your favorite sport? _____

9. What careers or occupations are you most interested in learning about? _____

_____

10. Do you prefer working:

    ❑ alone

    ❑ with one other student

    ❑ with a group of other students

    ❑ with adults

11. Imagine you could spend a lot of time at school doing something that was designed especially for you. Choose three categories listed below that would appeal to you the most. Number your choices in the following way:

1 = my first choice; 2 = my second choice; 3 = my third choice

_____ research something that interests me

_____ create something new or design and build an invention

_____ work on building my vocabulary

_____ publish stories or poems

_____ do puzzles and play strategy or logic games

_____ work on unique art projects

_____ do science experiments

_____ analyze historical events or learn about our government

_____ focus on a career study

_____ do a literature study

_____ work with mathematics

_____ study other countries

_____ study a foreign language

_____ be involved in acting, debating, or speech making

_____ compose music

_____ read more stories

_____ other: _____

                    _____

                    _____

Sample Letter to Parent(s)

Dear Parent(s):

I enjoy being _____'s (student's name) teacher. _____ has exhibited outstanding abilities in several academic areas and it is my desire to give _____ the opportunity to work on materials that would be more relevant to his or her abilities. I would also like to target specific skills: communication, creative thinking, critical thinking, higher-level thinking, inquiry, leadership, problem solving, and research and independent study. These skills will continue to be important throughout _____'s academic, professional, and personal life.

So that we can work together to better meet _____'s academic needs, I would like to set up an appointment with you and _____ to introduce a program called *Passport to Learn*, which is designed to meet the needs of high-potential students. During this meeting, I would like to review several goals that I have set for _____. I would also like to present you and _____ with a wide range of self-directed, self-paced, and independent activities from *Passport to Learn* that should appeal to _____. We will also review the management system for this program.

Please call me soon to arrange for a time that would be suitable for all of us to meet together. I look forward to making this year exciting and meaningful for _____.

Sincerely,

Checking In

Goals Inventory

Teacher: _____ Date: _____

Student name: _____

Because this student has high learning potential, I would like to expand his/her horizons this (circle one:) marking period, semester, trimester, year by working on goals that have been checked on this list.

Communication Skills

❑ The learner will be given the opportunity to engage in different types of writing:

   ❑ book reports   ❑ poetry

   ❑ reports or essays   ❑ short stories

   ❑ journals   ❑ speeches

   ❑ plays   ❑ writing directions

   ❑ other _____

❑ The learner will be given a variety of publishing opportunities.

❑ The learner will be given the opportunity to make use of the computer and other technology as productive tools.

Creative-Thinking Skills

❑ The learner will be given the opportunity to participate in activities that involve divergent thinking.

❑ The learner will be given the opportunity to complete activities that require:

   ❑ fluency (a large number of responses)

   ❑ flexibility (organize responses into categories)

   ❑ originality (uniqueness)

   ❑ elaboration (adding detail and/or explanation)

❑ The learner will be given the opportunity to engage in activities that require brainstorming techniques and generating his or her own ideas.

Critical-Thinking Skills and Higher-Level-Thinking Skills

❑ The learner will be given the opportunity to use focusing skills to define problems and set goals.

❑ The learner will be given the opportunity to use information-gathering skills by observing and questioning.

❑ The learner will be given the opportunity to use organizational skills by arranging information so it can be used more effectively:

   ❑ comparing: noting similarities and differences

   ❑ classifying: grouping according to common attributes

   ❑ ordering: sequencing information

❑ The learner will be given the opportunity to use analysis skills to examine information in detail.

❑ The learner will be given the opportunity to use generating skills to add new information:

   ❑ inferring: reasoning beyond available information to fill in gaps

   ❑ predicting: anticipating or forecasting future events

   ❑ elaborating: adding meaning to new information and linking it to existing information

Passport to Learn © 2001 Zephyr Press, Tucson, Arizona • 800-232-2187 • www.zephyrpress.com

❑ The learner will be given the opportunity to use integrating skills to connect and combine information.

❑ The learner will be given the opportunity to use evaluating skills to assess the reasonableness and quality of ideas:

    ❑ establishing criteria: setting standards for making judgments

    ❑ verifying: confirming the accuracy of information

    ❑ identifying errors: recognizing logical fallacies

Inquiry Skills

❑ The learner will be given the opportunity to develop inquiry skills by:

    ❑ making observations and generating questions about these observations

    ❑ selecting questions to investigate

    ❑ making predictions or hypothesis

    ❑ developing a procedure to test the hypotheses

    ❑ recording results from the data collected

    ❑ stating conclusions that tell what the results of the investigation mean

    ❑ recording questions, observations, and suggestions for future investigations

Leadership Skills

❑ The learner will develop his or her role as a leader by participating in leadership opportunities and:

    ❑ serving as a group facilitator

    ❑ making decisions and solving problems

    ❑ planning, setting goals, developing timelines, and evaluating results

    ❑ working on community projects

    ❑ being involved in simulations

    ❑ working with a mentor

Problem-Solving Skills

❑ The learner will be given the opportunity to engage in the process of Creative Problem-Solving by learning:

    ❑ fact finding

    ❑ problem finding

    ❑ idea finding

    ❑ solution finding

    ❑ acceptance finding

❑ The learner will be given the opportunity to engage in higher-level mathematical problem solving.

❑ The learner will be given the opportunity to participate in academic and creative competitions.

Research and Independent-Study Skills

❑ The learner will be taught how to research and organize information by using:

    ❑ surveys

    ❑ interviews

    ❑ card catalog

    ❑ Internet

    ❑ note cards

❑ The learner will be given the opportunity to produce a product or performance from the research.

❑ The learner will be given the opportunity to share results (findings, products, or projects) of an independent study with an appropriate audience.

Checking in at the Gate GOALS

Student/Parent/Teacher Conference

Teacher: _____ Date: _____

Student: _____

Because _____ (insert student's name) exhibits high learning potential, I would like to expand his/her horizons this (circle one: marking period, semester, trimester, year) by working on the following goals and skills:

_____ (insert student's name) will be given the opportunity to (list goals and skills):

_____

_____

_____

_____

_____

_____

_____

_____

_____

_____

These goals will be addressed as _____ works on the following *Tickets for Success*.

	Flight Number	Skills Addressed
1.	_____	_____
2.	_____	_____
3.	_____	_____
4.	_____	_____
5.	_____	_____
6.	_____	_____
7.	_____	_____
8.	_____	_____
9.	_____	_____
10.	_____	_____

Passport to Learn © 2001 Zephyr Press, Tucson, Arizona • 800-232-2187 • www.zephyrpress.com

Setting the Stage

Now that you have determined who will participate in the *Passport to Learn* program, set out your new *Travel Agent's Deskplate*. Pass out *Flight Attendant Buttons*, found on the following pages, to parent helpers, if available.

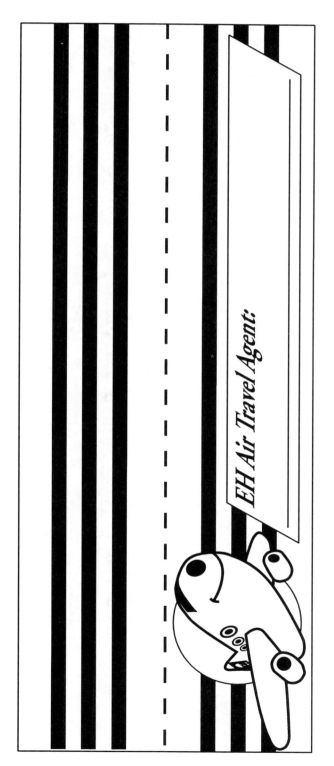
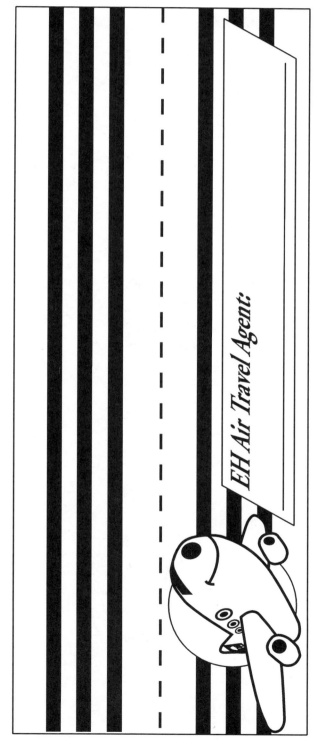

Flight Attendant Buttons

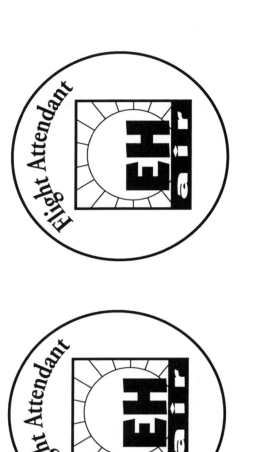

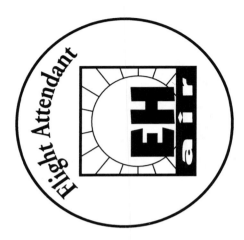

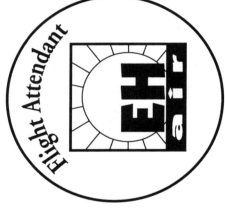

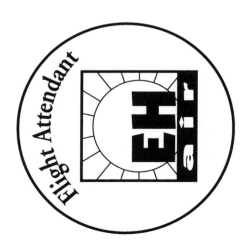

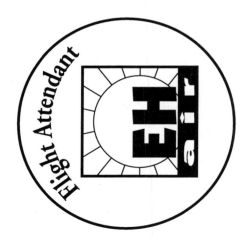

Chapter 3

Making Travel Plans

Preparing the Student Traveler

- 5 Departure Screens
- Passport Application
- Ticket Jacket
- Frequent-Flyer Miles Map
- Suitcase

"From your parents you learn love and laughter and how to put one foot before the other. But when books are opened you discover you have wings."

—Helen Hayes

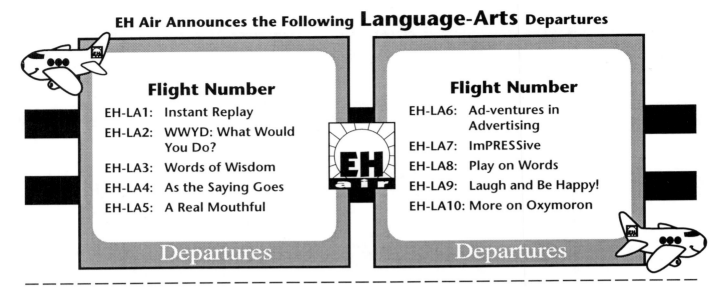

EH Air Announces the Following **Language-Arts** Departures

Flight Number

EH-LA1: Instant Replay

EH-LA2: WWYD: What Would You Do?

EH-LA3: Words of Wisdom

EH-LA4: As the Saying Goes

EH-LA5: A Real Mouthful

Flight Number

EH-LA6: Ad-ventures in Advertising

EH-LA7: ImPRESSive

EH-LA8: Play on Words

EH-LA9: Laugh and Be Happy!

EH-LA10: More on Oxymoron

Departures   Departures

Look over the Language Arts *Tickets for Success* choices and brief descriptions written below. Check off those that interest you, and then give this *Departures* page to your teacher.

❑ **EH-LA1—Instant Replay**
Learn about and write palindromes and palindromic phrases. *Skills: creative thinking, problem solving*

❑ **EH-LA2—WWYD: What Would You Do?**
Write your own "Choose Your Own Adventure" story. *Skills: creative and critical thinking, problem solving, communication*

❑ **EH-LA3—Words of Wisdom**
Study famous and not so famous quotations. Make your own quotation book. *Skills: creative thinking, communications, higher-level thinking, research*

❑ **EH-LA4—As the Saying Goes . . .**
Write fairy tales using jargon and clichés. *Skills: creative thinking, research*

❑ **EH-LA5—A Real Mouthful**
Create a dictionary of "big" words. *Skills: creative and critical thinking, higher-level thinking, inquiry, research*

❑ **EH-LA6—Ad-ventures in Advertising**
Advertise a new product by writing and producing a magazine or newspaper ad, a web page, and radio and TV commercials. *Skills: creative and critical thinking, higher-level thinking, communication, research*

❑ **EH-LA7—ImPRESSive**
Write a class newspaper. *Skills: creative and critical thinking, inquiry, communication*

❑ **EH-LA8—Play on Words**
Have fun with wordplay, such as alliteration, idioms, spoonerisms, Tom Swifties, and so on. *Skills: creative and critical thinking, research, inquiry*

❑ **EH-LA9—Laugh and Be Happy!**
Write and publish many types of humor. *Skills: creative thinking, higher-level thinking*

❑ **EH-LA10—More on Oxymoron**
Read about and write oxymora and pleonasms. *Skills: creative thinking, higher-level thinking*

Traveler's Name: _____

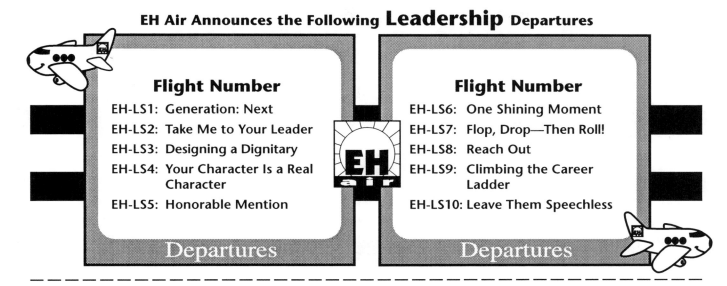

EH Air Announces the Following **Leadership** Departures

Flight Number

EH-LS1: Generation: Next

EH-LS2: Take Me to Your Leader

EH-LS3: Designing a Dignitary

EH-LS4: Your Character Is a Real Character

EH-LS5: Honorable Mention

Flight Number

EH-LS6: One Shining Moment

EH-LS7: Flop, Drop—Then Roll!

EH-LS8: Reach Out

EH-LS9: Climbing the Career Ladder

EH-LS10: Leave Them Speechless

Departures · Departures

Look over the Leadership *Tickets for Success* choices and brief descriptions written below. Check off those that interest you, then give this *Departures* page to your teacher.

❏ **EH-LS1—Generation: Next**
Survey and interview adults about their thoughts on leadership in the second millennium. *Skills: research, communication, inquiry*

❏ **EH-LS2—Take Me to Your Leader**
Study and present information about a past or present leader. *Skills: research, communication*

❏ **EH-LS3—Designing a Dignitary**
Design the perfect leader and give a presentation. *Skills: creative and critical thinking, problem solving, communication*

❏ **EH-LS4—Your Character Is a Real Character**
Write a story about your invented leader as you study character development. *Skills: creative and critical thinking, problem solving, communication*

❏ **EH-LS5—Honorable Mention**
Design an Honor Society recognizing students for outstanding achievements. *Skills: critical thinking, higher-level thinking, communication, leadership*

❏ **EH-LS6—One Shining Moment**
Describe a modern-day hero and how he or she uses lifeskills. *Skills: communication, critical thinking, inquiry, research*

❏ **EH-LS7—Flop, Drop—Then Roll!**
Write an essay about gifted people who have failed, made mistakes, and overcome obstacles. *Skills: critical thinking, higher-level thinking, inquiry, leadership*

❏ **EH-LS8—Reach Out**
Perform community service or take on a social action project. *Skills: communication, critical thinking, higher-level thinking, research, leadership*

❏ **EH-LS9—Climbing the Career Ladder**
Study a career, write a resume and cover letter, and demonstrate a skill needed for your career. *Skills: critical thinking, research, communication, leadership*

❏ **EH-LS10—Leave Them Speechless**
Write speeches to inform, persuade, and entertain. *Skills: critical and creative thinking, communication, leadership*

Traveler's Name: _____

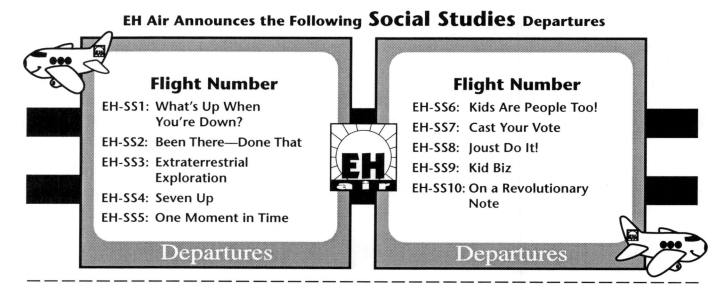

EH Air Announces the Following **Social Studies** Departures

Flight Number

EH-SS1: What's Up When You're Down?

EH-SS2: Been There—Done That

EH-SS3: Extraterrestrial Exploration

EH-SS4: Seven Up

EH-SS5: One Moment in Time

Flight Number

EH-SS6: Kids Are People Too!

EH-SS7: Cast Your Vote

EH-SS8: Joust Do It!

EH-SS9: Kid Biz

EH-SS10: On a Revolutionary Note

Departures   Departures

Look over the Social Studies *Tickets for Success* choices and brief descriptions written below. Check off those that interest you, then give this *Departures* page to your teacher.

❑ **EH-SS1—What's Up When You're Down?**
Study a country in the Southern Hemisphere and design a brochure. *Skills: creative thinking, inquiry, research, communication*

❑ **EH-SS2—Been There—Done That**
Find objects or artifacts for each of the destination cities, then design a futuristic artifact. *Skills: research, higher-level thinking*

❑ **EH-SS3—Extraterrestrial Exploration**
Describe a newly discovered extraterrestrial society. Create an artifact for the society and a product persuading people to move to the planet. *Skills: creative thinking, research, higher-level thinking*

❑ **EH-SS4—Seven Up**
Study the Seven Wonders of the Ancient World, then decide on natural and modern world wonders. *Skills: research, higher-level thinking*

❑ **EH-SS5—One Moment in Time**
Create a time capsule that will be opened 100 years from now. *Skills: creative and critical thinking, research, higher-level thinking*

❑ **EH-SS6—Kids Are People Too!**
Write a Bill of Rights for Children. *Skills: creative and critical thinking, research, higher-level thinking*

❑ **EH-SS7—Cast Your Vote**
Design a new political party and develop a campaign. *Skills: creative and critical thinking, research*

❑ **EH-SS8—Joust Do It!**
Research castles, make a castle diorama or model, and study heraldry to make a coat of arms. *Skills: creative thinking, research, higher-level thinking*

❑ **EH-SS9—Kid Biz**
Develop a plan for starting your own business. *Skills: creative and critical thinking, research*

❑ **EH-SS10—On a Revolutionary Note**
Study wartime songs and compose your own song about wars. *Skills: creative thinking, research, higher-level thinking*

Traveler's Name: _____

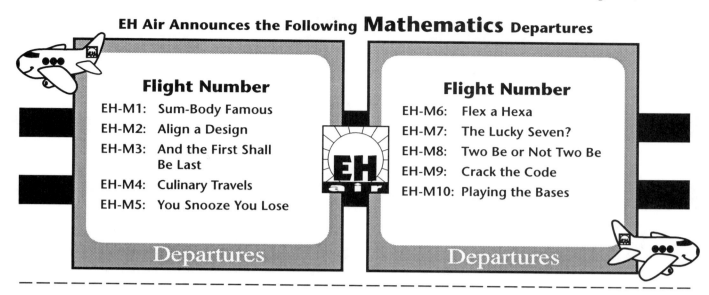

EH Air Announces the Following **Mathematics** Departures

Flight Number

EH-M1: Sum-Body Famous

EH-M2: Align a Design

EH-M3: And the First Shall
Be Last

EH-M4: Culinary Travels

EH-M5: You Snooze You Lose

Departures

Flight Number

EH-M6: Flex a Hexa

EH-M7: The Lucky Seven?

EH-M8: Two Be or Not Two Be

EH-M9: Crack the Code

EH-M10: Playing the Bases

Departures

Look over the Mathematics *Tickets for Success* choices and brief descriptions written below. Check off those that interest you and give this *Departures* page to your teacher.

❑ **EH-M1—Sum-Body Famous**
Study a famous mathematician. *Skills: research, communication, critical thinking*

❑ **EH-M2—Align a Design**
Create fractals, such as a Sierpinski triangle and a Von Koch's snowflake. *Skills: research, critical and creative thinking*

❑ **EH-M3—And the First Shall Be Last**
Discover palindromes in three-digit numbers. *Skills: problem solving*

❑ **EH-M4—Culinary Travels**
Study food and recipes from around the world. *Skills: research, problem solving, creative thinking*

❑ **EH-M5—You Snooze You Lose**
Design your own "dream" bedroom. *Skills: research, problem solving, creative and critical thinking*

❑ **EH-M6—Flex a Hexa**
Create a hexa-hexa-flexagon. *Skills: research, problem solving, creative thinking*

❑ **EH-M7—The Lucky Seven?**
Investigate the stock market and follow seven stocks for a month. *Skills: critical thinking, inquiry, research*

❑ **EH-M8—Two Be or Not Two Be**
Learn how the binary system works and amaze your friends with a base-2 puzzle. *Skills: creative thinking, inquiry, problem solving, research*

❑ **EH-M9—Crack the Code**
Write secret codes using binary, octal, and hexadecimal number systems. *Skills: research, critical thinking, problem solving*

❑ **EH-M10—Playing the Bases**
Develop an argument for a new number system such as base 12 or the dozenal system. *Skills: research, critical thinking, problem solving*

Traveler's Name: _____

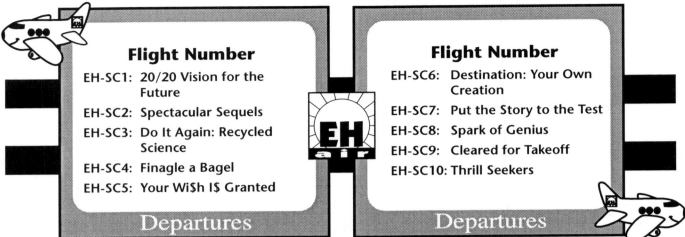

EH Air Announces the Following **Science** Departures

Flight Number

EH-SC1: 20/20 Vision for the Future

EH-SC2: Spectacular Sequels

EH-SC3: Do It Again: Recycled Science

EH-SC4: Finagle a Bagel

EH-SC5: Your Wi$h I$ Granted

Flight Number

EH-SC6: Destination: Your Own Creation

EH-SC7: Put the Story to the Test

EH-SC8: Spark of Genius

EH-SC9: Cleared for Takeoff

EH-SC10: Thrill Seekers

Departures

Departures

Look over the Science *Tickets for Success* choices and brief descriptions written below. Check off those that interest you, then give this *Departures* page to your teacher.

❑ **EH-SC1—20/20 Vision for the Future**
Solve overpopulation problems in the year 2020. *Skills: problem solving, creative thinking*

❑ **EH-SC2—Spectacular Sequels**
Invent something new or improved. *Skills: problem solving, creative thinking*

❑ **EH-SC3—Do It Again: Recycled Science**
Develop scientific equipment and materials using 35mm film canisters. *Skills: research, problem solving, creative thinking*

❑ **EH-SC4—Finagle a Bagel**
Conduct experiments using bagels. *Skills: research, problem solving, creative thinking*

❑ **EH-SC5—Your Wi$h I$ Granted**
Enter a scientific contest. *Skills: research, inquiry, creative thinking, critical thinking*

❑ **EH-SC6—Destination: Your Own Creation**
Design a space colony on Mars. *Skills: creative and critical thinking, higher-level thinking*

❑ **EH-SC7—Put the Story to the Test**
Develop scientific experiments for young children that connect literature and science. *Skills: creative and critical thinking, research, inquiry*

❑ **EH-SC8—Spark of Genius**
Research four scientific topics and create an electric board for each using the scientific vocabulary. *Skills: creative and critical thinking, research, inquiry*

❑ **EH-SC9—Cleared for Takeoff**
Create a paper airplane contest. *Skills: creative and critical thinking, research, inquiry*

❑ **EH-SC10—Thrill Seekers**
Design your own amusement park. *Skills: creative and critical thinking, research, inquiry*

Traveler's Name: _____

Passport to Learn © 2001 Zephyr Press, Tucson, Arizona • 800-232-2187 • www.zephyrpress.com

Passport Application

Expanding Horizons

Name: _____ Date: _____

Birthdate: _____ Birthplace: _____

Height: _____ Hair Color: _____ Eye Color: _____

Please include a 1½" x 1½" photo of yourself when you submit this application (or draw a self-portrait).

• •

By applying for a *Passport to Learn* with Expanding Horizons Airlines and signing this application, you agree to follow these guidelines while working on *Tickets for Success:*

❑ I will stay on task when given the opportunity to work on Expanding Horizons *Tickets for Success* during class.

❑ I will assume responsibility for producing quality work.

❑ I will assume responsibility for completing each Expanding Horizons *Ticket for Success* within a mutually agreed upon time frame.

❑ I will assume responsibility for assisting with accurate record keeping when working on and completing assignments, products, and projects.

❑ I will assume responsibility for finishing all requirements on each *Ticket for Success* that I have agreed to complete.

❑ I will assume responsibility for doing a self-evaluation of completed assignments, products, and projects.

❑ I will be responsible, ethical, and courteous when using the Internet.

❑ I will be respectful of the learning styles of all students in my class.

Student Signature: _____ Date: _____

Teacher Signature: _____ Date: _____

Parent Signature: _____ Date: _____

Ticket Jacket

Expanding Horizons Airlines

Originating Flight		
1. Airline	Flight	Destination Date
Connecting Flight(s)		
2. Airline	Flight	Destination Date
3. Airline	Flight	Destination Date
4. Airline	Flight	Destination Date
5. Airline	Flight	Destination Date
6. Airline	Flight	Destination Date
7. Airline	Flight	Destination Date
8. Airline	Flight	Destination Date
9. Airline	Flight	Destination Date
10. Airline	Flight	Destination Date

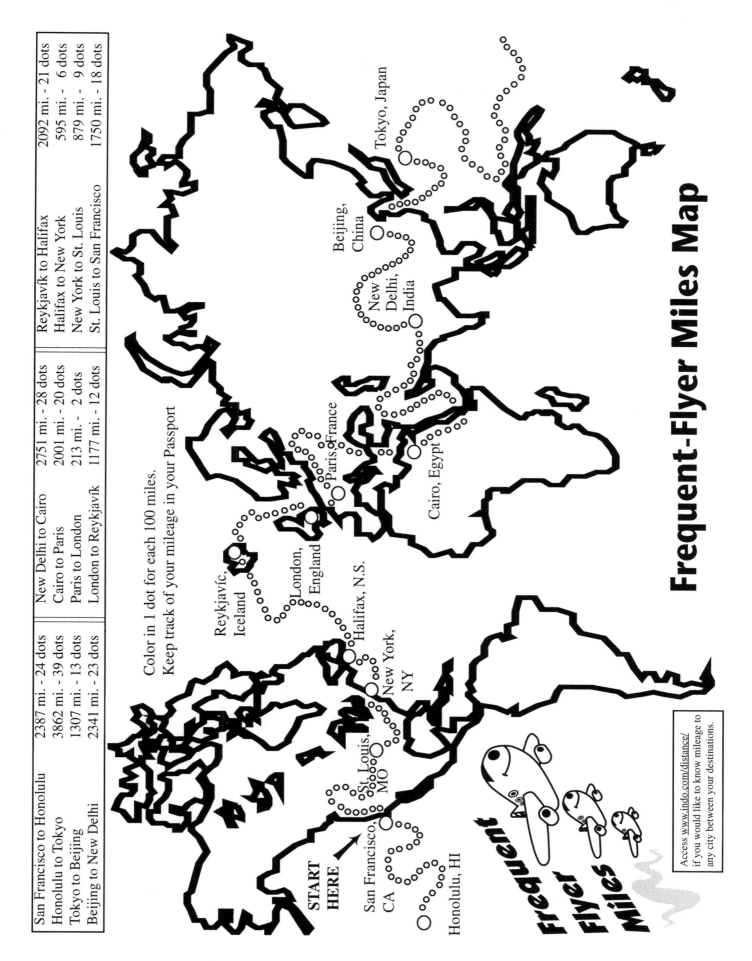

Frequent-Flyer Miles Map

Color in 1 dot for each 100 miles.
Keep track of your mileage in your Passport

San Francisco to Honolulu	2387 mi. - 24 dots	New Delhi to Cairo	2751 mi. - 28 dots	Reykjavík to Halifax	2092 mi. - 21 dots
Honolulu to Tokyo	3862 mi. - 39 dots	Cairo to Paris	2001 mi. - 20 dots	Halifax to New York	595 mi. - 6 dots
Tokyo to Beijing	1307 mi. - 13 dots	Paris to London	213 mi. - 2 dots	New York to St. Louis	879 mi. - 9 dots
Beijing to New Delhi	2341 mi. - 23 dots	London to Reykjavík	1177 mi. - 12 dots	St. Louis to San Francisco	1750 mi. - 18 dots

Tokyo, Japan

Beijing, China

New Delhi, India

Paris, France

Cairo, Egypt

Reykjavíc, Iceland

London, England

Halifax, N.S.

New York, NY

St. Louis, MO

START HERE

San Francisco, CA

Honolulu, HI

frequent flyer Miles

Access www.indo.com/distance/ if you would like to know mileage to any city between your destinations.

Suitcase Cover for Project Folders

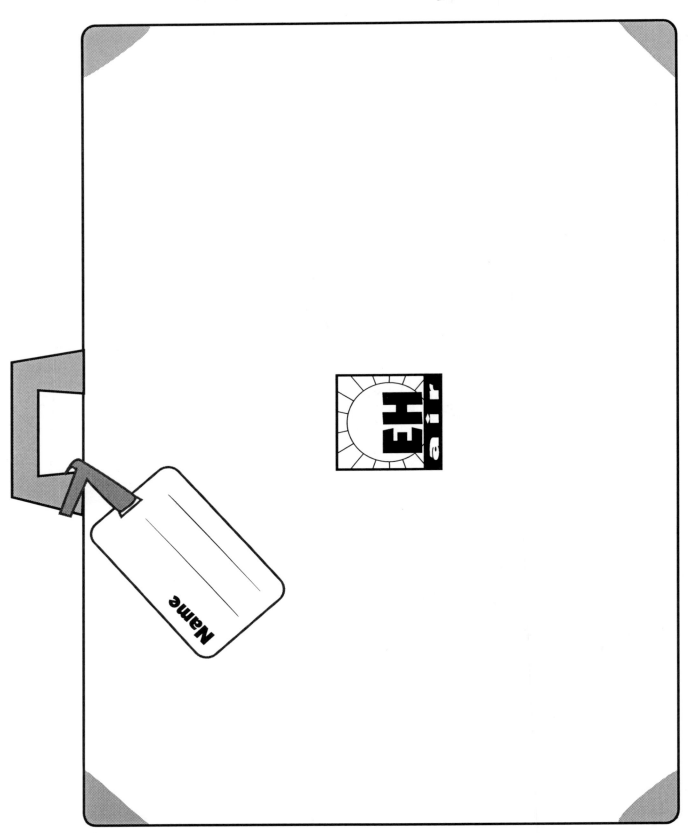

Passport to Learn © 2001 Zephyr Press, Tucson, Arizona • 800-232-2187 • www.zephyrpress.com

Chapter 4

Necessities for the Student Traveler

Preparing the Student Traveler

- Passport
- Flight Log
- Destination City Passport Stamps
- Certificate of Completion

"The greatest gifts you can give your children are the roots of responsibility and the wings of independence."

—Denis Waitley

Assembling the *Passport*

The *Passport* is made up of three pages. To assemble the *Passport*, follow the steps below:

1. Fold each page on Line A.

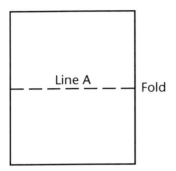

2. With the fold on top of the pages, fold each page on Line B.

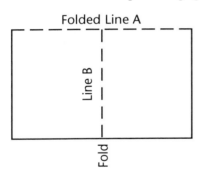

3. The folds should now be at the top and on the left side of each page.

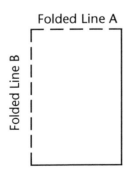

4. When *Passport* pages are folded as shown in step 3, the small page numbers 3 and 5 should be on top of each of the folded pages.

5. Now, insert small page number 3 inside of small page number 2. Then insert small page number 5 inside of small page number 4.

6. The small *Passport* pages should now be in order from page 1 through page 12.

New York,
USA

St. Louis,
Missouri,
USA

Your
Photo
Here

Name:
Birthdate: Birthplace:
Height   Hair: Eyes:
Issue Date:
Expiration Date:
Signature:

11

2

Line A

Line B

Expanding Horizons

Passport

London, England

Paris, France

Date	Flight Number	Miles Earned	Total Miles	Destination City-When Reached

Reykjavík, Iceland

Halifax, Nova Scotia

Date	Flight Number	Miles Earned	Total Miles	Destination City-When Reached

Passport to Learn © 2001 Zephyr Press, Tucson, Arizona • 800-232-2187 • www.zephyrpress.com

Beijing, China

Honolulu, Hawaii, USA

Tokyo, Japan

San Francisco, California USA

7

9

8

5

New Delhi, India

Cairo, Egypt

Date	Flight Number	Miles Earned	Total Miles	Destination City-When Reached

Using the Passport

Once frequent-flyer miles are gathered, the *Passport* should be filled out by the student in the following manner:

- First column: Record the date when the student has completed a *Ticket for Success* and it has been evaluated.

- Second column: Record the flight number for the *Ticket for Success* that has just been completed.

- Third column: Record the frequent-flyer miles earned for that *Ticket for Success,* as found on the last page of the *Flight Log* (see page 44).

- Fourth column: Tally the total number of frequent-flyer miles as they accumulate.

- Fifth column: This column will only be used when a destination city is reached. Record the name of the city when the student has reached or surpassed a city. For example, after starting in San Francisco and when the student has accumulated at least 2,387 total frequent-flyer miles, he or she can record *Honolulu* in the Destination City column. Note, it may take two or three projects to reach Honolulu.

Passport to Learn © 2001 Zephyr Press, Tucson, Arizona • 800-232-2187 • www.zephyrpress.com

Flight Log

Itinerary Planner and Evaluation

Traveler's Name: _____

Ticket Flight Number: _____

NOTE: One *Flight Log* must be completed for each *Ticket for Success*.

Priorities for Planning

Earn *Frequent-Flyer Miles* the fastest way by making planning a priority as you complete a *Ticket for Success*. Read the *Ticket for Success* carefully and follow the itinerary. As you plan, stay on course by following the *Flight Plan* listed below and by recording information in this *Flight Log*.

1. Choose a *Ticket for Success*.

2. Keep all of the information you gather while working on your *Ticket for Success* in your *Suitcase*.

3. *Chart Your Course* and set goals using the next page.

4. Keep track of your time on task as you work on the *Ticket for Success* itinerary.

5. Write down information you already know about the *Ticket for Success* topic.

6. Write down what you hope to learn about the *Ticket for Success* topic.

7. Ask yourself probing questions.

8. Gather information using books, magazines, CD-ROMs, videos, interviews, Internet sources, and so on.

9. Keep track of resources.

10. Organize your information in a written document.

11. Produce your product.

12. Write your presentation.

13. Practice your presentation.

14. Present your speech and product to an appropriate audience.

15. Evaluate your learning, writing, project, and presentation.

16. Record the number of *Frequent-Flyer Miles* you receive in your *Passport* and on your *Frequent-Flyer Miles Map*.

Charting Your Course

Goals: Read your *Ticket for Success* carefully and set goals for what you must do to complete the itinerary.

ETA: Write down the date when you expect to complete each goal.

Student questions or comments: As you work on each goal, write down questions that you would like to ask your teacher when you meet for a check-in.

Teacher questions or comments: Your teacher will record questions and comments here when you meet for a check-in.

Check-in: Each time you meet with your teacher, write the date here. Also, you and your teacher should initial this box when a check-in is completed.

Goals	ETA	Student Questions or Comments	Teacher Questions or Comments	Check-In Date and Initials

Time on Task

As you work on your *Ticket for Success*, keep track of the amount of time you spend each day and what you accomplish. Make sure you stay on task when you are given time to work on your *Ticket for Success*.

Date	Amount of Time Spent Today	Today I Accomplished . . .

What I Know

Determine what you already know about your *Ticket for Success* topic. Record that information below.

- _____
- _____
- _____
- _____
- _____

What I Want to Learn

Think about what you would like to learn about your *Ticket for Success* topic. Record questions and ideas below.

- _____
- _____
- _____
- _____
- _____

Probing Questions

Ask yourself probing questions about your *Ticket for Success* topic. The questions below will help to get you started. What additional questions do you have? Use the back of this page to record your thoughts.

- What event or idea do I want to explain to others?
- What do people already know?
- What confusions do people have about this topic?
- How can I clear up these confusions or contradictions?
- How can I best present information about this topic so that people will understand it clearly?

Use the following format when citing your resources. Attach a bibliography to your written work. All references should be alphabetized by the last name of the author (if none given, use the first word of the title, disregarding words such as *A*, *An*, or *The*).

Note: On any of the entries, if you are unable to find a piece of information listed in these examples, simply skip that part of the entry and move on.

Books

Author (last name first). Title (underlined). City where the book is published: Publisher, Copyright date. Example: Manning, Jerry. <u>1000 Airlines in Color</u>. Stillwater, Minn.: Voyageur Press, 1999.

Magazines

Author (last name first). "Article Title." (in quotation marks) <u>Title of the Magazine</u> (underlined or italicized) Date (month year): page numbers of the article. Example: Mazur, Sara. "What a Great Time to be Flying." *Plane and Pilot Magazine* May 2000: 65–68.

Encyclopedias

"Article title" (in quotation marks). Title of the reference book (underlined) Vol. No. City where published: Publisher, copyright date: pages used. Example: "Airplanes." <u>World Book Encyclopedia</u> Vol. 1. New York, N.Y.: World Book, Inc., 1998: 136–138.

Films, Slides, Video Tapes

Title (underlined). Type of material (film, video, slides). Production Company, date. Time length. Example: <u>Pioneers of Aviation</u>. Video. Columbia River Entertainment, 1998. 300 minutes.

Interviews

Person (last name first, person's title). Person's job title. City and state where interview took place. Type of interview. Day Month Year. Example: Yaeger, Chuck. General. U.S. Army officer. New York, N.Y. Telephone interview. 4 January 2001.

World Wide Web

Author. <u>Title of item</u> (underlined). <u>http://address/filename</u> (underlined). Date of document or download. Example: Schultz, Alex. <u>My World: Origami and Planes</u>. <u>http://www.geocities.com/CapeCanaveral/Runway/6095/origami.html</u>. 16 May 2000.

Electronic Sources

Author. "Article Title" (in quotation marks). <u>Product name</u> (underlined). Computer software. City where published: Company name, Date. CD-ROM. Example: Jones, Anne. "Aerospace Engineers." <u>Info-trac</u>. Computer software. Novato, Calif.: Software Tools Works, 1994, CD-ROM.

 Passport to Learn © 2001 Zephyr Press, Tucson, Arizona • 800-232-2187 • www.zephyrpress.com

Report/Essay Checklist

As you write your report or essay, ask yourself the following questions. Also have a parent or friend edit your report or essay and ask these questions while editing. Make corrections where necessary.

- ❑ Is the paper clear and focused?
- ❑ Does the paper hold the reader's attention?
- ❑ Does the organization of the paper flow smoothly from introduction to body to conclusion?
- ❑ Are the transitions between ideas thoughtful and smooth?
- ❑ Is the introduction to the paper inviting?
- ❑ Do details seem to fit where they are placed?
- ❑ Is the conclusion satisfying?
- ❑ Are the words specific and accurate?
- ❑ Do the words and phrases that are used create pictures in your mind?
- ❑ Is the title original, and does it capture the central theme of the piece?
- ❑ Is spelling correct?
- ❑ Is punctuation accurate?
- ❑ Is there thorough understanding and consistent application of capitalization skills?
- ❑ Are grammar and usage correct?
- ❑ If handwritten, is handwriting legible, with uniform spacing between words?
- ❑ If word processed, is there appropriate use of fonts and font sizes?
- ❑ Is this piece ready to publish?

Product Checklist

You will produce a product for most of the *Tickets for Success*. Suggested products are given on the *Ticket for Success*, but if you have a better idea, you may implement it. Check the *Product Ideas* in this *Flight Log* to help you think of ideas. When you finish producing your product, ask yourself the following questions:

- ❑ Is my product relevant?
- ❑ Does my product enhance my written document and/or my presentation?
- ❑ Is my product creative?
- ❑ Are the words on my product easy to read?
- ❑ Are the words free of spelling or grammatical errors?

Product Ideas

A
Advertisement
Advice column
Alphabet book
Autobiography

B
Ballad
Billboard
Biography
Board game
Brochure
Bumper sticker

C
Cartoon
Carving
Case study
Chart
Code and/or cipher
Collage
Collection
Commercial
Community service project
Computer graphics
Computer program

D
Dance
Definitions
Demonstration
Design
Diary
Diorama

E
Editorial
Electric board
Epitaph
Experiment

F
Fable
Folktale
Fractured fairy tale

G
Graph
Greeting card

H
Handbook
Horoscope
How-to book or speech
HyperStudio® presentation

I
Illustration
Interest inventory
Interview
Invention

J
Jingle
Journal

L
Legend
Lesson plan
Letters
Logic puzzle

M
Mad-libs
Map
Mind Map
Mobile
Model
Mural
Musical composition
Musical performance
Musical video
Myth

N
Newsletter
Newspaper article
Novel
Nursery rhyme

O
Opposing views essay
Oral report
Origami

P
Painting
Pantomime
Parody
Pattern story

Play
Poem
Pop-up book
Portfolio
Poster
PowerPoint® presentation
Proverbs
Puppet show

Q
Questionnaire

R
Rap
Reader's theater
Research paper
Review (book, movie, restaurant, etc.)
Role play

S
Science project
Scrapbook
Sculpture
Simulation
Skit
Slide show
Song
Speech
Spreadsheet
Story
Survey

T
Tall tale
Test
Time line

V
Venn diagram
Video

W
Webpage

Presentation Checklist

Practice your presentation in front of an audience (parents or friends). Use this self-evaluation checklist as you practice.

- ❑ Can everyone in the audience hear you?
- ❑ Are you showing interest and enthusiasm?
- ❑ Are you speaking at an appropriate rate?
- ❑ Are you varying the pitch of your voice, not speaking in monotone?
- ❑ Are you careful not to use filler words (uhm, uh, ah, mm, like)?
- ❑ Are you making eye contact with the audience?
- ❑ Are you speaking to the entire audience, not just one or two people?
- ❑ Are you using good posture and keeping your hands and feet calm?
- ❑ Are you using gestures that add to the presentation and have a purpose?
- ❑ Are you confident and well prepared?
- ❑ Are you using your notes sparingly?
- ❑ Is your presentation of an appropriate length—not too long or too short?
- ❑ Is your presentation organized with an introduction, body of information, and conclusion?
- ❑ Have you given appropriate support and elaboration to the main idea?
- ❑ Is it clear that you are an expert on the subject?
- ❑ Will your audience learn something new?

If you are using a technological presentation tool such as HyperStudio® or PowerPoint® for your presentation, use the checklist below to evaluate your use of the technology.

- ❑ Do you have a slide for each of your key points?
- ❑ Have you varied the transitions between the slides?
- ❑ Have you added sounds and/or music to the presentation?
- ❑ Have you used colors, patterns, and designs that are appealing and creative?
- ❑ Does each slide show originality?
- ❑ Have you used a mix of pictures, animations, and graphics?
- ❑ Have you focused on the content of your presentation not the glitz of the technology?

Evaluation

The maximum *Frequent-Flyer Miles* that can be earned for each item is shown in parentheses. Your score for each item can range from 0 up to the maximum number of miles indicated.

Frequent-Flyer Miles Earned

	Self-Evaluation	Teacher Evaluation

❑ Did you follow the suggested *Flight Plan?* Can you explain your plan to your teacher? (up to 100 miles)
Comments:

❑ Did you think about and write down what you wanted to learn, and did you ask probing questions? What questions? (up to 100 miles)
Comments:

❑ Did you keep track of your time on task? (up to 100 miles)
Comments:

❑ Did you use a variety of resources? Are resources listed properly? (up to 200 miles)
Comments:

❑ Did you organize your information? (up to 100 miles)
Comments:

❑ Did you produce a well-written document using the correct writing mechanics? (up to 400 miles)
Comments:

❑ Did you make an extraordinary project? (up to 400 miles)
Comments:

❑ Did you present your research and project in a superior manner? (up to 400 miles)
Comments:

❑ Did you evaluate your efforts? (up to 200 miles)
Comments:

TOTAL
Note: Multiply total by 2 if this is a 4,000-mile ticket. Multiply total by 3 if this is a 6,000-mile ticket.

Passport Stamps

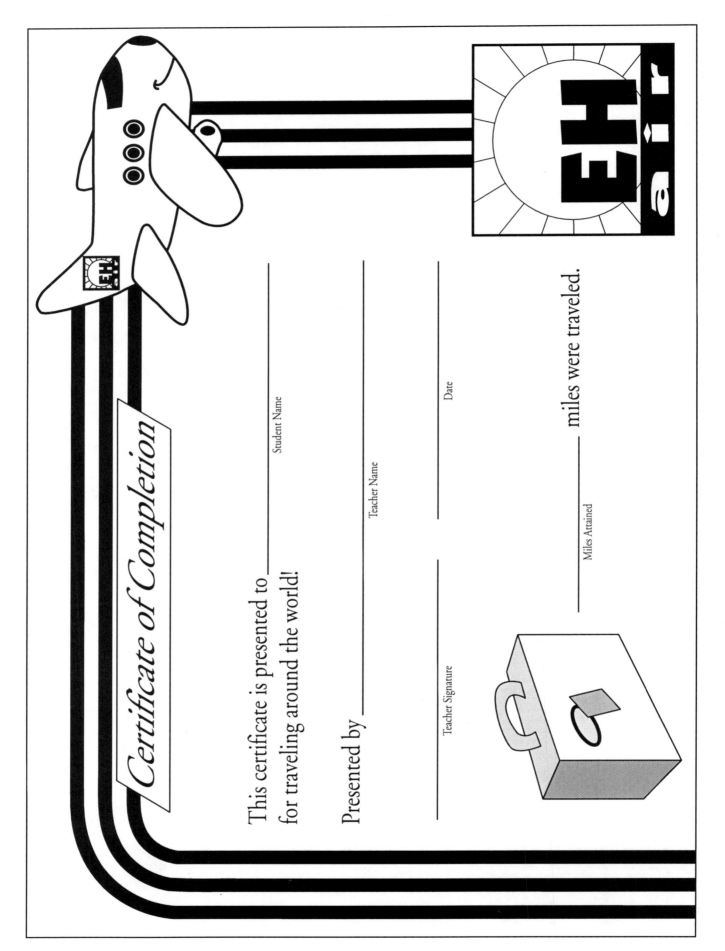

Certificate of Completion

This certificate is presented to _____

for traveling around the world!

Student Name

Presented by _____

Teacher Name

_____
Teacher Signature

_____
Date

_____ miles were traveled.

Miles Attained

EH air

Chapter 5

Expanding Horizons
Tickets for Success

Language Arts

Ticket for Success

Flight # EH-LA1

Itinerary: Instant Replay

1. Read about palindromes on Boarding Pass EH-LA1.

2. Do further research on palindromes. Report your findings to your class by explaining what palindromes are, telling the history of palindromes, and giving some examples. Give at least five facts about palindromes and their history and offer at least five examples of palindromes.

3. Write five to seven phrases that are palindromes and add pictures to illustrate them. If available, read the book, *Sit on a Potato Pan, Otis!: More Palindromes*, by Jon Agee, for ideas.

4. Palindromes in Mathematics: Practice your addition by taking a two-digit number (no duplicate digits allowed, such as 22, 33, and so on), reverse the number, then add the numbers together. Continue this until the number becomes a palindrome. Example: 46 + 64 = 110, 110 + 011 = 121 (121 is a palindrome). Use the chart in Boarding Pass EH-LA1 to do this assignment.

5. Extension: Research additional information about palindromes related to mathematics. Investigate three-digit palindromes. See Boarding Pass EH-M3 (page 121).

Departure Date: _____ **ETA:** _____

Mileage Perks: *Up to ★2,000 Frequent-Flyer Miles★*

Destination Skills: *creative thinking and problem solving*

Boarding During: *Mathematics and Language Arts*

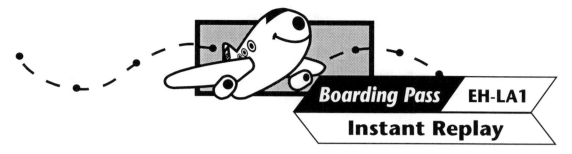

Boarding Pass / EH-LA1
Instant Replay

Palindromes: A palindrome is a word or phrase that reads the same in both directions (forward and backward). Some simple examples are:

LEVEL   EVE   RACECAR   RADAR

The longest single English word in common usage that is a palindrome is *redivider*. In Finnish, there is a 25-letter palindromic word: *solutomaattimittaamotulos*, which means the result from a measurement laboratory for tomatoes.

When creating reversible phrases, it is commonly accepted that punctuation and word spacing can be ignored, as in this famous palindromic phrase: *Madam, I'm Adam.* Three other famous palindromic phrases are: *Was it a car or a cat I saw?* and *A man, a plan, a canal—Panama* and *Able was I ere I saw Elba* (Napoleon's palindrome).

Find out more about palindromes using the following references:
Keyword: **Palindromes**
website: http://www.fun-with-words.com
Book: *Sit on a Potato Pan, Otis!: More Palindromes*, by Jon Agee

Palindromes in Mathematics: All numbers can be changed into a *palindromic sum*. For example, take a number (87), reverse the digits of the number (78), then add the numbers together (87 + 78 = 165); repeat this process until you get a *palindromic sum* (165 + 561 = 726, 726 + 627 = 1353, 1353 + 3531 = 4884). 4884 is a *palindromic sum*.

Complete the following chart to find the palindromic sums of two-digit numbers.

The total of the two-digits must equal this sum	Example	Palindrome	Number of steps it took to become a palindrome
between 3 and 9	23 + 32 = 55	55	1
10	46 + 64 = 110 110 + 011 = 121	121	2
11			
12			
13			
14			
15			
16			
17 *			
18			

Note: When the total of the digits = 17 (98 or 89), it takes 24 steps to produce a palindrome.

Ticket for Success

Flight # EH-LA2

Itinerary: WWYD: What Would You Do?

1. Read a published "Choose Your Own Adventure" story to understand how this type of story is designed.

2. Study the flowchart on Boarding Pass EH-LA2 to understand how to design your own "Choose Your Own Adventure" story.

3. Get index cards from your teacher and label each index card to correspond with the flowchart.

4. Write a rough draft of your "Choose Your Own Adventure" story. If you are having difficulty thinking of an idea, use the Story Starter Ideas on Boarding Pass EH-LA2. Edit your rough draft with a peer, then conference with your teacher and/or parent before writing your final draft.

5. Add illustrations and/or graphics to your story.

6. Complete your story in book form, or for something special, create a HyperStudio® or PowerPoint® presentation. One index card equals one HyperStudio® card or PowerPoint® screen. Create buttons that allow your readers to make different story choices.

Departure Date: _____ **ETA:** _____

Mileage Perks: *Up to ★2,000 Frequent-Flyer Miles★*

Destination Skills: *creative and critical thinking, problem solving, and communication*

Boarding During: *Language Arts or Computer Lab*

Passport to Learn © 2001 Zephyr Press, Tucson, Arizona • 800-232-2187 • www.zephyrpress.com

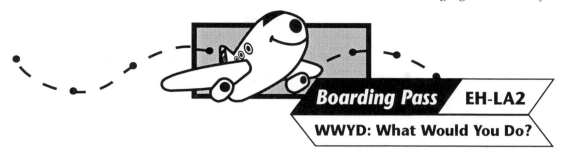

"Choose Your Own Adventure" Story Flowchart

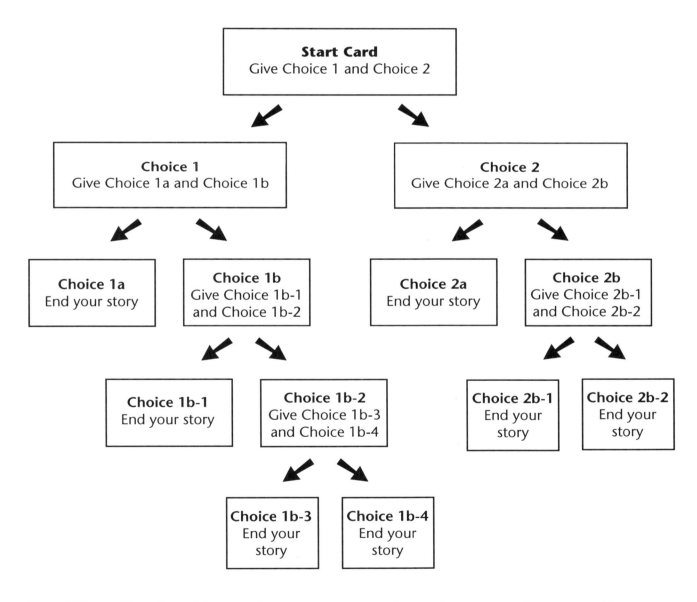

Start Card
Give Choice 1 and Choice 2

Choice 1
Give Choice 1a and Choice 1b

Choice 2
Give Choice 2a and Choice 2b

Choice 1a
End your story

Choice 1b
Give Choice 1b-1
and Choice 1b-2

Choice 2a
End your story

Choice 2b
Give Choice 2b-1
and Choice 2b-2

Choice 1b-1
End your story

Choice 1b-2
Give Choice 1b-3
and Choice 1b-4

Choice 2b-1
End your
story

Choice 2b-2
End your
story

Choice 1b-3
End your
story

Choice 1b-4
End your
story

Note: "Choose Your Own Adventure" story structures can be much more complex as you add more choices and fewer endings. This is the best structure for your first time of writing such a story!

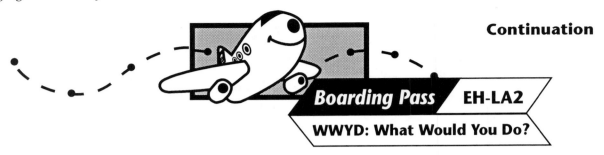

Continuation

Boarding Pass / **EH-LA2**

WWYD: What Would You Do?

Story Starter Ideas

The post office delivered a package on which was stamped, "Handle with Care." Suddenly a noise came from the package . . .

One day I was walking through my neighborhood when I came upon . . .

I never expected that one day, I'd open my Trapper Keeper® and find . . .

He didn't look like a famous scientist; he looked more like . . .

Five seconds left on the scoreboard clock—until . . .

I was home alone when suddenly the doorbell rang and . . .

One minute I was riding my skateboard, the next thing I knew I was . . .

When I picked the round, smooth object from the tree, I discovered it was . . .

A mosquito as large as a small dog buzzed in my ear . . .

After 20 days, I wondered if it would ever stop raining . . .

As usual, school started in September, but this time . . .

Something strange happened to my parents. The only word they could speak was, "Yes!" Now I could ask . . .

I changed places with my parents for a day and . . .

I woke up and suddenly my dreams had come true. I was now . . .

My most prized possession is my . . .

Disaster! All of the television stations had stopped broadcasting for the rest of the month. Now I had to . . .

I worry about many things. Most of all, I worry about . . .

When I looked up, the jack-o'-lantern smiled at me . . .

It was too still and quiet. That could only mean that . . .

I turned the key on the Time Machine and suddenly I was . . .

Note: You can use Chris Van Allsburg's book, *The Mysteries of Harris Burdick*, for visual story starters.

Or, think of your own story starters for your "Choose Your Adventure" story!

 For an example of a "Choose Your Own Adventure" story about the underground railroad, check the following website: www.nationalgeographic.com/features/99/railroad/j1.html.

Ticket for Success

Flight # EH-LA3

Itinerary: Words of Wisdom

Favorite quotations are often very meaningful to us. We enjoy some quotations because they put a grin upon our face, others enlighten and comfort us, and still others motivate us, inspire us, and encourage creative thinking.

1. Read quotations from various resources. See Boarding Pass EH-LA3 for sources.

2. Form a collection of at least 30 of your favorite quotations.

3. Publish your favorite quotations (those that mean the most to you) in a creative format. Suggestions are listed below:

    *   Make an *ABC Book* of your favorite quotations.

    *   Make a book of *Daily Quotations* for a month (or maybe a year).

    *   Illustrate some of your favorite quotes by creating a painting or a mural, by creating a cartoon version of the quotations, or by drawing pictures and adding captions to explain what the quotations mean.

4. Extension: Do something for your community that will inspire others through quotations, such as designing quotation bookmarks for the local library or place mats for a local restaurant.

Departure Date: _____ **ETA:** _____

Mileage Perks: *Up to ★ 2,000 Frequent-Flyer Miles ★*

Destination Skills: *creative thinking, communication, higher-level thinking, and research*

Boarding During: *Language Arts or Reading*

Boarding Pass / EH-LA3

Words of Wisdom

Quotation Websites

The Quotations Home Page:
http://www.geocities.com/~spanoudi/quote.html

The Quotations Page:
http://www.starlingtech.com/quotes/

A Dictionary of Scientific Quotations:
http://naturalscience.com/dsqhome.html

Famous Quotes and Quotations:
http://www.startingpage.com/html/
quotations.html

Quoteland:
http://www.quoteland.com/

The Quotation Guide:
http://life.bio.sunysb.edu/ee/msr/quote.html

Mark Twain Quotations:
http://www.twainquotes.com/

Familiar Quotations:
http://www.bartleby.com/99/index.html

Famous Quotations Network:
http://www.famous-quotations.com/

Quotation Center:
http://www.cybernation.com/victory/quota-
tions/directory.html

Quotation Depot:
http://www.quotationdepot.com/

Quotations and Sayings Database:
http://www.btinternet.com/~alexandergrant/
quotes/index.htm

Books of Quotations

Available at the library, bookstores, and online:

In Our Own Words: A Treasury of Quotations from the African-American Community, by Eliza Dinwiddie-Boyd

Shakespeare Quotations, compiled by G. F. Lamb

Brewer's Quotations: A Phrase and Fable Dictionary, by Nigel Rees

Chambers Dictionary of Quotations, edited by Alison Jones

A Treasury of Jewish Quotations, compiled by Joseph L. Baron

A Collection of Familiar Quotations, compiled by John Bartlett

Encyclopedia of the Great Quotations, compiled by Lyle Stuart

A Yearning Toward Wildness: Environmental Quotations, edited by Tim Homan

A Treasury of Great American Quotations, compiled by Charles Hurd

The Writer and the Reader: A Book of Literary Quotations, compiled by Neil Ewar

Reflections on Childhood: A Quotations Dictionary, compiled by Irving and Anne D. Weiss

Cat Quotations: A Collection of Lovable Cat Pictures and Best Cat Quotes, edited by Helen Exley

Best Quotations for All Occasions, edited by Lewis C. Henry

Think of quotations by famous people and characters from books, television, and movies. Use quotations from your parents, friends, and family. Think of your own original and unique quotations.

Ticket for Success

Flight # EH-LA4

Itinerary: As the Saying Goes . . .

Jargon can mean nonsensical and meaningless talk, or the specialized or technical language of a trade, profession, or similar group. A *cliché* is a commonly used expression or idea. Many times, jargon and clichés are overused. Consider, for example, sports commentary: *It's a nip-and-tuck game. That really silenced the crowd. You can feel the momentum swinging. It's a game of inches. They're not out of it yet. Swing and a miss. That one's going, going, gone!*

1. Research various trades, professions, sports, and so on. Make a list of jargon and clichés in at least five different categories. You can find information on the Internet, in trade books, cliché books, or by asking people you know.

2. Reread your favorite fairy tale.

3. Rewrite your tale in three to five different ways using jargon and clichés from the professions or groups you have listed. Examples from *Little Red Riding Hood* are written on Boarding Pass EH-LA4.

4. Illustrate your new creations.

Departure Date: _____ **ETA:** _____

Mileage Perks: *Up to ★★4,000 Frequent-Flyer Miles★★*

Destination Skills: *creative thinking, research*

Boarding During: *Language Arts*

Boarding Pass / EH-LA4

As the Saying Goes . . .

Excerpts from Various Versions of *Little Red Riding Hood* Using Jargon and Clichés

From a fancy cooking magazine perspective:

Since Little Red's grandmother is not feeling well, Little Red decides to prepare something for grandmother to delight her with culinary and creative pleasures. Grandmother would certainly enjoy fresh pastries, prepared individually with the freshest ingredients. Little Red carries these delicious treats to grandmother in a basket, woven from the finest reeds and willow branches available from the banks of the local river. Along the way to grandmother's house, Little Red Riding Hood picks edible flowers and culinary herbs to turn any leftover scraps of dough that Grandmother might have in her refrigerator into delectable little treats. Little Red uses her map, which is made of hardy materials, as an interesting, durable tablecloth, upon which the two dine for lunch.

From a football game announcer's perspective:

The woodsman entered Grandmother's house and delivered a hit to the wolf that really cleaned his clock. The wolf really got his bell rung there. It looks like we've got a wolf shaken up. We hate to speculate on the injury . . . (but we will anyway).

From a travel agent's perspective:

Act quickly to reserve a seat with EH Travels for our exciting and suspenseful Red Riding Hood adventure. Your all-inclusive three-day trip will include airfare, all meals, plus complementary tours and passes for retracing the fairy-tale expedition of Little Red Riding Hood. A world-class botanist will lead a nature tour through the mysterious and beautiful deep, dark forest where Little Red traveled. You will visit and tour Grandma's charming cottage museum. Grandma, Little Red, the wolf, and the woodsman are sure to drop in for a surprise visit. You'll be able to witness firsthand the change in the wolf's behavior. Call for your reservations today!

From a radio disc jockey's perspective:

Instead of listening to the top 40 this morning, Mom was in the kitchen with my red cape. She told me that Grandma's signal is beginning to fade, and I'd better clear a time slot to visit her. I was beginning to fear that Mom might be broadcasting an emergency, so I quickly tuned in on her message and beamed into Grandma's house.

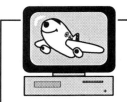

Use keyword: **cliches,** or check out clichés on these websites:

► http://www.westegg.com/cliche/
► http://www.sportscliche.com/

Ticket for Success

Flight # EH-LA5

Itinerary: A Real Mouthful

1. Create a dictionary using only "big" words. To be considered a "big" word, a word must have at least six syllables.

2. Each page should correspond to a letter of the alphabet, starting with *A* and ending with *Z*.

3. Every page of your dictionary should contain at least three words. Your first word for *A* might be *Abecedarian*. Look up the word to see what it means.

4. Include the definition for each word and use the word in a sentence.

5. Illustrate some of the words in your alphabet book and put your book together in an interesting format.

6. Note: All words in your book must be found in the *Webster New World Dictionary* (or other standard dictionary of your teacher's choice).

7. Extension: Give learning hints that would help your friend remember a word and its meaning. See Boarding Pass EH-LA5 for ideas.

8. Extension: Make a subject-specific dictionary for math, science, or any other subject.

Departure Date: _____ **ETA:** _____

Mileage Perks: *Up to ★2,000 Frequent-Flyer Miles★*

Destination Skills: *creative and critical thinking, higher-level thinking, inquiry, and research*

Boarding During: *Language Arts*

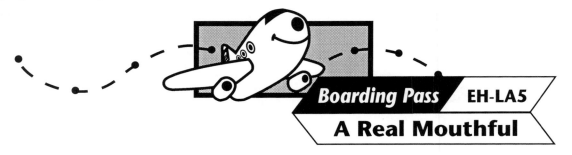

Boarding Pass / EH-LA5

A Real Mouthful

Learning Hints

How can you help others learn words that are difficult to understand or remember? A few ideas are listed below.

1. **Use visual vocabulary hints.**
    Examples:

    Dwindle Dilate | Inscribe |

2. **Make up a musical jingle or rhyme to remember a word and its meaning.**
    Example: the meaning of *satiate*:

    > *Why, it's quite great!*
    > *It means to fill up, as with food,*
    > *and to put someone in a good mood,*
    > *to satisfy a need—*
    > *quite a good word indeed!*

3. **Use a mathematical or logical hint.**
    Example: Show the addition of prefixes and suffixes.

    dis + taste + ful + ness
    dis + taste + ful + ly

4. **Try spatial hints.**
    Example: Draw a picture of a capitol building with the "O" forming the dome.

5. **Use mnemonics to spell difficult words and remember tricky meanings.**
    Examples:
    ▶ Separate is A RAT of a word to spell.
    ▶ The principal is your PAL.
    ▶ To use the word PLEase is a princiPLE that one should always follow.
    ▶ Stalactites: They hang on *tite*. Stalactites hang onto the ceiling of a cave.

Passport to Learn © 2001 Zephyr Press, Tucson, Arizona • 800-232-2187 • www.zephyrpress.com

Ticket for Success

Flight # EH-LA6

Itinerary: Ad-ventures in Advertising

1. Read about persuasion, gimmicks, and propaganda on Boarding Pass EH-LA6.

2. Using old magazines, find an example of each of the propaganda techniques or gimmicks that are listed on Boarding Pass EH-LA6. Make a booklet out of these examples.

3. Think of a new product to "sell" to your classmates. Examples: a new cereal, gum, or backpack.

4. Design a logo, slogan, and packaging for your new product.

5. Use your logo, slogan, and/or packaging in advertisements that you create for your product. Use propaganda techniques and gimmicks to launch a promotional campaign. See Boarding Pass EH-LA6 for steps.

   • Write and draw a magazine or newspaper advertisement for your product.

   • Write and produce (on videotape or the computer) a 30-second television commercial for your product.

   • Design a web page for your product.

   • Write and produce a 15-second radio commercial on audiotape.

6. Write a one-page essay on how learning to recognize propaganda techniques can help you decide whether or not to purchase the next new item that appears on the market.

Departure Date: _____ **ETA:** _____

Mileage Perks: *Up to ★★★ 6,000 Frequent-Flyer Miles ★★★*

Destination Skills: *creative and critical thinking, research, communication, higher-level thinking*

Boarding During: *Language Arts or Computer Lab*

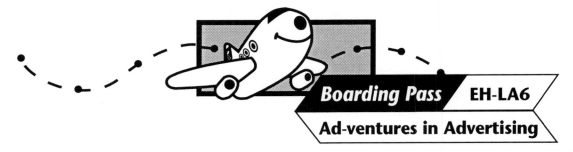

Boarding Pass / **EH-LA6**

Ad-ventures in Advertising

The Power of Persuasion

Propaganda techniques generally used in advertisements:

1. **Bandwagon:** The desire to join the crowd or be on the winning side. Additional persuasion techniques associated with the bandwagon approach are:
   - **Sex appeal:** A knockout teenage girl says she drinks milk for beautiful hair and a super smile.
   - **Snob appeal:** The reader or viewer is urged to be like the elite.
   - **Appeal to excellence:** Only the best is good enough for the reader or viewer.
   - **Plain folk:** Reverse snob appeal. Good down-home cooking; nothing fancy, but good enough for Aunt Maggie; like Grandma used to make, and so on.
   - **Patriotism:** The consumer will be showing American values.

2. **Testimonial:** The desire to identify with those who seem more important, knowledgeable, or famous than we are:
   - Using a television star, well-known athlete, or famous public figure to endorse an item.

3. **Repetition:** The product name is repeated at least four times.

4. **Emotional words:** Words that will make you feel strongly about someone or something. Examples:
   - new, fantastic, gorgeous
   - eat a particular cereal brand to prevent cancer

5. **Humor:** California Raisins, cartoons, jokes, Energizer® bunny

Brainstorm ideas for your advertisements here:

_____

_____

_____

_____

_____

_____

_____

Passport to Learn © 2001 Zephyr Press, Tucson, Arizona • 800-232-2187 • www.zephyrpress.com

Ticket for Success

Flight # EH-LA7

Itinerary: ImPRESSive!

1. Write a class newspaper and include the following:

   - **Front page:** News stories about the major things that are happening in your class or in your school right now.

   - **Editorial page:** Voice your opinion about things that happen at your school. Make sure you clear your editorial with your teacher before you publish it.

   - **Sports page:** Interview your physical education teacher and your playground supervisors to get some ideas on what sports seem to be the most popular, how students could do a better job of following the rules of sports and games, additional playground equipment that is needed on your playground, and so on.

   - **Features section:** You might include comic strips, a school fashions page, advice column, reviews, puzzles, and so on.

   - **Financial page:** Let students know the costs of things that are coming up: yearbook, lunch money, agenda books, and so on.

   - **Advertising:** If approved by your teacher or principal, you might want to get a few local businesses to fund the printing of your paper. Make sure that you include an advertisement for those businesses in your paper.

2. Publish your paper using a computer word-processing or desktop-publishing program.

3. Boarding Pass EH-LA7 will give you suggestions for writing news articles.

Departure Date: _____ **ETA:** _____

Mileage Perks: *Up to ★★4,000 Frequent-Flyer Miles★★*

Destination Skills: *creative and critical thinking, inquiry, communication*

Boarding During: *Language Arts*

Boarding Pass / **EH-LA7**

ImPRESSive!

Tips for Good Reporting

- Get information for news stories by asking the *5W and How* questions: *Who? What? When? Where? Why? How?*
- Be objective. Do not state your own opinion. Use quotations to express others' opinions. Take notes when you interview so that you know you are quoting people accurately.
- Use active words. Instead of "The air *was filled* with smoke." Write "The smell of smoke *filled* the air."

Reporters' Duties

- Outline the purpose of the article first
- Research and interview
- Write the article
- Proofread and edit the article
- Rewrite the article
- Type the article on the computer
- Spell check the article

Structure for Articles

First Paragraph

- Give the basic information in your first one or two sentences.
- Make sure you answer the 5W and How questions.
- Hook the reader at the beginning with a:
    - a. funny, clever, or surprising statement
    - b. question
    - c. provocative statement

Second Paragraph

- Add supporting details.
- Include quotations from people you have interviewed.

Last Paragraph

- Add details of lesser importance.
- End with a quote or a catchy phrase.
- Do not say "In conclusion . . ." or "To end this article . . ."

Headline Tips

- Use just a few strong, active words.
- Make sure that the headline is consistent with the story.
- Be creative; use humor or a clever phrase.
- Use wordplay to contribute to the meaning, not to show off. Example, *Poultry in Motion* is an informative headline for an article about a tipped truck dumping thousands of chickens

Ticket for Success

Flight # EH-LA8

Itinerary: Play on Words

1. Have fun with words by investigating word play. Read Boarding Pass EH-LA8 to learn about different types of wordplay.

alliterations	pangram
anagrams	spoonerism
hyperbole	stink-pinks
idioms	stinky-pinky
malapropisms	Tom Swifties
net lingua	tongue twisters
onomatopoeia	word equations
oxymora	

2. Make a book entitled *Just for Laughs*, and give the definition, the history, and three to five examples for each type of wordplay listed above.

3. Boarding Pass EH-LA8 lists Internet sources to get you started on your research.

Departure Date: _____ **ETA:** _____

Mileage Perks: *Up to ★2,000 Frequent-Flyer Miles★*

Destination Skills: *creative and critical thinking, research, inquiry*

Boarding During: *Language Arts*

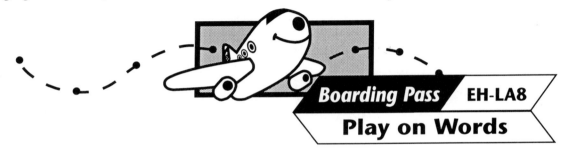

Boarding Pass / **EH-LA8**

Play on Words

Alliteration: The occurrence in a phrase or line of speech or writing of two or more words having the same initial sound. Example: <u>w</u>ailing in the <u>w</u>inter <u>w</u>ind

Anagram: A word or phrase formed by reordering the letters of another word or phrase. Example: The earthquakes—That queer shake

Idiom: A speech form or expression of a given language that is nonsense if it is taken literally or that cannot be understood from the individual meanings of its words. Example: "As easy as pie," meaning very easy

Hyperbole: An exaggeration or extravagant statement not meant literally used as a figure of speech. Examples: "I could sleep for a year." "This book weighs a ton."

Malapropism: A ludicrous misuse of a word. Example: It's chucked full.

Net lingua: Acronyms and smileys that are used almost exclusively on the Internet. Example: A net lingua acronym: BFN = bye for now; a net lingua smiley: :-)

Onomatopoeia: The formation or use of words that imitate in sound what they denote. Examples: buzz, cuckoo

Oxymoron: A phrase with words that contradict each other. Example: cruel to be kind.

Pangram: A series of words that contains all the letters of the alphabet. Example: The quick brown fox jumps over the lazy dog.

Spoonerism: An unintentional transposition of sounds of two or more words. Example: "Let me sew you to your sheet" for "Let me show you to your seat."

Stink-pink or **Stinky-pinky:** Two rhyming words of one syllable, the last word is usually a noun, and the first word modifies it. Examples: rare hare = unusual rabbit, or witty kitty = clever cat

Tom Swifty: A play on words that always follows the same pattern. There is a pun between the meaning of an adverb and what a speaker has said. Example: "I know who turned off the lights," Tom hinted darkly.

Tongue twister: Combining the effects of alliteration, particularly of similar but not identical sounds, with a phrase designed so that the speaker slips easily when saying the phrase quickly. Example: "Peter Piper picked a peck of pickled peppers."

Word equation: An equation that represens a word or phrase. Examples: *26 = L of the A* means: 26 letters of the alphabet; *7 = W of the A.W.* means: 7 Wonders of the Ancient World

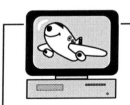

Check the following websites:
▶ http://www.members.home.net/teachwell/index.htm
▶ http://www.fun-with-words.com
▶ http://www.wolinskyweb.com/word.htm

Ticket for Success

Flight # EH-LA9

Itinerary: Laugh and Be Happy!

1. Learn how to write poems that make you smile or laugh. Pattern poems, such as acrostic poems, cinquains, diamanté, and limericks are good forms to use when writing humorous poems. Write at least one of each of these types of poems. Boarding Pass EH-LA9 explains how to compose several types of poems.

2. Write at least one joke and riddle.

3. Draw at least one cartoon and one caricature.

4. Put all of your ideas together in a *Laugh and Be Happy* book. Make sure your book does not put down others. Remember that a sense of humor means to laugh and be playful without hurting others.

5. Use a computer word-processing or desktop-publishing program to put your book in final format.

6. If you are pleased with your final product, send your book to a publisher. See Boarding Pass EH-LA9 for addresses, phone numbers, and websites.

Departure Date: _____ **ETA:** _____

Mileage Perks: *Up to ★★4,000 Frequent-Flyer Miles★★*

Destination Skills: *creative thinking, higher-level thinking*

Boarding During: *Language Arts, Reading, or Computer Lab*

Boarding Pass / EH-LA9

Laugh and Be Happy!

Types of Poems	Example
Acrostic poems: Letters of a special word are written vertically, then each letter of the special word begins a line of the poem, written horizontally, giving meaning to the word.	**A**erodynamically built for **I**nternational and continental flights. **R**unways busy, taking **P**assengers to exciting and intriguing new **L**ands and offering **A**dventures, **N**orth or south **E**ast or west!
Cinquain: An unrhymed form of poetry with five lines. 　　Line 1: The topic in two-syllable word or words 　　Line 2: four syllables, describing the topic 　　Line 3: six syllables, expressing action 　　Line 4: eight syllables, expressing feeling 　　Line 5: two syllables, a synonym for the topic	*Airplane* *Silvery bird* *Jetting across the sky* *Glittering like a shooting star* *Flying*
Diamanté: A diamond-shaped poem with seven lines. It either develops one topic or starts out with one topic then starts to change in the middle to the antonym of the topic. 　　Line 1: A noun 　　Line 2: Two adjectives describing the noun 　　Line 3: Three verbs or -*ing* action words 　　Line 4: A four-word phrase about the topic 　　Line 5: Three verbs or -*ing* action words for the ending noun 　　Line 6: Two adjectives describing the ending noun 　　Line 7: A noun, either a synonym of the first line or an antonym of the first line.	*Airplane* *Sleek, serene* *Lifting, climbing, cruising* *Navigating through the heavens* *Soaring, coasting, landing* *Graceful, feathery* *Bird*
Limerick: A five-line poem; lines 1, 2, and 5 rhyme, and lines 3 and 4 rhyme. Lines 1, 2, and 5 have three beats, and lines 3 and 4 have two beats.	*The flying vacation express,* *Can cause a vacationer stress.* *You're packed in like sardines* *In designer blue jeans,* *And your clothes are not permanent press.*

Boarding Pass / **EH-LA9**

Laugh and Be Happy!

Where to Get Published

Publications

Merlyn's Pen Magazine
fiction, essays, poetry; grades 6–12
P.O. Box 1058
East Greenwich, RI 02818
800-247-2027
website: http://www.merlynspen.com
e-mail: merlynspen@aol.com

Potato Hill Poetry
poems, exercises, artwork, essays; grades
K–12
81 Speen Street
Natick, MA 01760
1-888-5-POETRY
website: http://www.potatohill.com
e-mail: info@potatohill.com

Cobblestone Publishing Company
drawings, poems, letters, book reviews;
contact for upcoming themes and deadlines
30 Grove St., Suite C
Peterborough, NH 03458
Fax: 603-924-7380
website: http://cobblestonepub.com/pages/
kidstht.htm
e-mail: custsvc@cobblestone.mv.com

Stone Soup
stories, poems, book reviews, and art by
young people through age 13
P.O. Box 83
Santa Cruz, CA 95063
800-447-4569
website: http://www.stonesoup.com
e-mail: (for foreign contributors only)
editor@stonesoup.com

Creative with Words Publications
poetry, prose, and artwork; school-aged
children
P.O. Box 223226
Carmel, CA 93922
Fax 831-655-8627
website: http://members.tripod.com/
CreativeWithWords
e-mail: cwwpub@usa.net

Children's Express
news reported and edited by kids
1331 H Street NW
Suite 900
Washington, DC 20005
202-737-7377
website: http://www.cenews.org

Young Authors Magazine
anthology program; essays, short stories, and
poems
3015 Woodsdale Blvd.
Lincoln, NE 68502-5053
402-450-1252
Fax: 402-421-9682
website: http://www.yam.regulus.com
e-mail: yam@regulus.com

Boarding Pass / **EH-LA9**

Laugh and Be Happy!

Online Publishing

Kids' Space
international Internet exchange of creative
activities; online submittal form
website: http://www.kids-space.org
e-mail: bulletin@ks-connection.org

Funhouse
story and poem exchange site; online
submittal form
website: http://liswa.wa.gov.au/funhouse
e-mail: Liskidz@mail.liswa.wa.gov.au

Achievement Awards

Scholastic Art and Writing Awards
annual awards for writing and art
555 Broadway
New York, NY 10012
212-343-6493
website: http://www.scholastic.com/
artandwriting/about.htm
e-mail: A&Wgeneralinfo@Scholastic.com

Ticket for Success

Flight # EH-LA10

Itinerary: More on Oxymoron

1. Read about oxymora (plural of oxymoron) on Boarding Pass EH-LA10.

2. Research oxymora on the World Wide Web. Sites are listed on Boarding Pass EH-LA10.

3. Read Jon Agee's book, *Who Ordered the Jumbo Shrimp?*

4. Illustrate at least 10 oxymora in a comic book format; *or*

5. Rewrite Jon Agee's book using at least 10 oxymora and illustrations of your own.

6. Pleonasms are the opposite of oxymora. Read about them on Boarding Pass EH-LA10.

7. Extension: Use HyperStudio® to write a story using oxymora and pleonasms. Each HyperStudio® card you create should have at least two buttons. One button leads to an oxymoron that ties into your story and the other button leads to a pleonasm that also connects to your story. Use at least five oxymora and five pleonasms. Have fun and be creative!

Departure Date: _____ **ETA:** _____

Mileage Perks: *Up to ★2,000 Frequent-Flyer Miles★*

Destination Skills: *creative thinking, higher-level thinking*

Boarding During: *Language Arts, Reading, or Computer Lab*

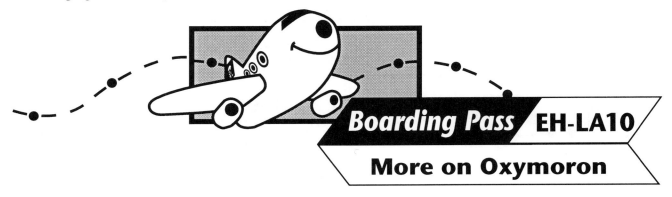

Boarding Pass / EH-LA10

More on Oxymoron

More on Oxymoron

Oxymora: An oxymoron is a literary figure of speech in which contradictory or opposite terms are combined. For example, one of the most common oxymora is "jumbo shrimp." Jumbo means very large, while shrimp means very small. The term "jumbo shrimp" indicates two opposite sizes. Other examples include the terms "pretty ugly," "clearly confused," "old news," "original copies," and "small crowd."

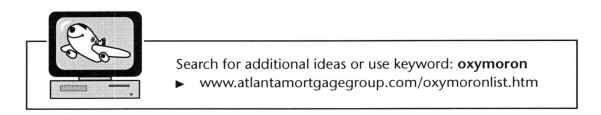

Search for additional ideas or use keyword: **oxymoron**
► www.atlantamortgagegroup.com/oxymoronlist.htm

Extra for Experts: Many people misuse the plural form of oxymoron thinking it should be spelled "oxymorons." Oxymoron is the singular form of the word. The plural of oxymoron is *oxymora.*

Pleonasms: Pleonasms are antonyms (opposites) of oxymora. A pleonasm consists of two words that are redundant (say the same thing). A pleonasm uses more words than necessary for the expression of a single idea. Examples would include expressions like "overabundant," "annual yearbook," "anonymous stranger," "climb up," and "exactly the same."

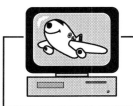

Search for additional ideas or use keyword: **pleonasm**
► http://www.wordexplorations.com/pleonasm.html

   Passport to Learn © 2001 Zephyr Press, Tucson, Arizona • 800-232-2187 • www.zephyrpress.com

Chapter 6

Expanding Horizons
Tickets for Success

Leadership Skills

Ticket for Success

Flight # EH-LS1

Itinerary: Generation: Next

1. You are the advisor to the governor of your state. Think about the problems that might take place in your state in this third millennium. Help your governor begin to solve these problems by interviewing adults in your community about at least one of the following questions:

   - What will be the greatest challenges for the school districts of your state?

   - What environmental problems will your state face?

   - How will technological advances affect business and industry in your state?

   - What challenges will confront the economy of your state?

   - How will the government of your state deal with issues in education, environment, technology, and the economy?

2. Using the issue you have chosen, design a survey with at least 10 questions related to your topic. Administer your survey to at least 10 adults. Use the survey and interview guides on Boarding Pass EH-LS1 to assist you in developing these instruments.

3. Review the results of your survey then create a one- to two-page written review, graphs/charts, and a presentation to share the results of your investigation and interview. Send a copy of your results to the governor of your state.

Departure Date: _____ **ETA:** _____

Mileage Perks: *Up to ★2,000 Frequent-Flyer Miles★*

Destination Skills: *research, communication, inquiry*

Boarding During: *Language Arts or Social Studies*

Passport to Learn © 2001 Zephyr Press, Tucson, Arizona • 800-232-2187 • www.zephyrpress.com

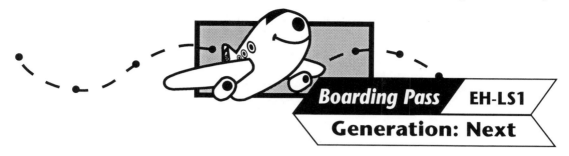

Boarding Pass **EH-LS1**

Generation: Next

Before the Interview:

1. Decide what information you most want to know. Below are the major topics you can choose from for your survey. Think of 10 questions that are closely related to the topic you choose. For instance, if you choose the education question, think of additional questions to ask about funding, test scores, teacher competency tests, violence, voucher systems, and so on.

   - What will be the greatest challenges for the school districts of your state?
   - What environmental problems will your state face?
   - How will technological advances affect business and industry in your state?
   - What challenges will confront the economy of your state?
   - How will the government of your state deal with issues in education, environment, technology, and the economy?

2. Write your 10 questions below, but phrase them as statements. Make a survey out of your questions, phrasing them so that the interviewees can state whether they *strongly agree, agree, disagree, strongly disagree,* or *are undecided.* Example: Lack of funding for public education will be the greatest challenge for our school districts. Follow up by asking why they feel this way.

   _____
   _____
   _____
   _____
   _____
   _____
   _____
   _____
   _____

3. Make appointments for each of your interviews and arrive on time.

During the Interview:

   - Be polite and patient. Give the interviewee time to answer each question. Take notes as the person answers your questions.
   - When asking a question, listen to the answer. If you are not sure you understand, ask additional questions.
   - If you are planning to quote the person directly during your presentation, it is best to ask permission from the interviewee.
   - Respect the interviewee's opinion, even if you disagree.
   - Make sure you thank the interviewee at the conclusion of the interview.

After the Interview:

   - Review your notes to be sure you understand them.
   - Write a summary immediately so you clearly remember what was said.

Ticket for Success

Flight # EH-LS2

Itinerary: Take Me to Your Leader

1. Choose a twentieth- or twenty-first century past or present leader to study, and write down at least three reasons why you chose to study this leader.

2. Research the leader of your choice and prepare to present the answers to the questions listed on Boarding Pass EH-LS2.

3. Use at least three references as you study this leader. Your local library will have biographies and autobiographies about your chosen leader. You can also find them at www.biography.com on the Internet.

4. Compile the information about your leader and answers to the questions into a series of cards for presentation or display (can be handwritten or computer generated).

5. Present your research to the class in three to five minutes. The presentation should be as creative and interesting as possible. Consider using HyperStudio® or PowerPoint® to assist you in your presentation.

Departure Date: _____ **ETA:** _____

Mileage Perks: *Up to ★2,000 Frequent-Flyer Miles★*

Destination Skills: *research, communication*

Boarding During: *Language Arts or Social Studies*

Key Questions about Your Leader

1. Give a brief description of your leader. Comment on the following:
   - family background and early life
   - interests and abilities
   - education and career
   - major contributions
   - challenges faced

2. Why was your leader admired?

3. Was there anything about your leader that caused people to dislike him or her?

4. What did you notice about your leader's creative and critical thinking skills?

5. What did you notice about your leader's communication skills?

6. What did you notice about your leader's "people" skills?

7. How was the world affected by your leader's contributions?

8. Compare and contrast your leader with another leader of your choice.

9. After studying your leader, do you admire this person any more or less? Why?

10. In what ways would you like to be like the leader you have chosen?

Several websites that will help you find information on famous leaders are:
- ▶ http://tlc.ai.org/fameamer.htm
- ▶ http://myhero.com/home.asp
- ▶ http://giraffe.org
- ▶ http://www.achievement.org/autodoc/pagegen/mainmenu.html?hb=1

If U.S. presidents interest you, a good website that will connect you to presidential libraries is:
- ▶ www.state.de.us/facts/ushist/uspres1.htm

Ticket for Success

Flight # EH-LS3

Itinerary: Designing a Dignitary

The most outstanding leaders of the world possess outgoing personal and social behaviors and a sound foundation of social and moral values.

1. Create a new leader that you feel would be respected by all because of his or her positive character traits. Be very specific. Use the suggestions on Boarding Pass EH-LS3 to get started.

2. Use the Venn diagram on Boarding Pass EH-LS3 to compare yourself to your new leader. How are you alike and different? Why would knowing this be important for you?

3. Use the suggested product ideas on Boarding Pass EH-LS3 to introduce your new leader to others. Use at least one product idea from each level listed on the Boarding Pass.

4. Take on the role of this dignitary and present yourself to your class in character. Consider using HyperStudio® or PowerPoint® to enhance your presentation about your new dignitary.

Departure Date: _____ **ETA:** _____
Mileage Perks: *Up to ★2,000 Frequent-Flyer Miles★*
Destination Skills: *creative and critical thinking, problem solving, communication*
Boarding During: *Language Arts or Social Studies*

Passport to Learn © 2001 Zephyr Press, Tucson, Arizona • 800-232-2187 • www.zephyrpress.com

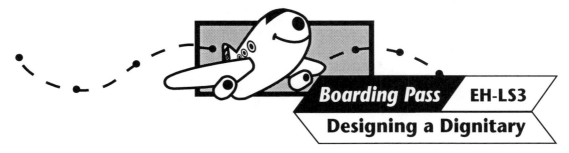

Boarding Pass / **EH-LS3**
Designing a Dignitary

Characteristics of Your Dignitary

- full name and nickname
- age
- gender
- height and weight
- type of body build
- skin tone, eye color, hair color, shape of face
- predominant features and distinguishing marks
- favorite music
- favorite food
- favorite types of clothing
- favorite school subject
- favorite sport and/or game
- favorite hobby
- favorite literature
- favorite expressions
- type of childhood

- first memory
- most important childhood event that still affects him/her
- education
- religion
- finances
- mother
- father
- siblings
- husband/wife
- relationship with each family member
- something your dignitary has always wanted to do
- something your dignitary would someday like to own
- your dignitary's heroes
- your dignitary's fondest wish

Digging Deeper

- What would your dignitary like to change about himself/herself?
- What do people like most about your dignitary?
- What do people like least about your dignitary?
- What are your dignitary's biggest accomplishments and biggest regrets?
- How does your dignitary handle conflict, problems, and change?

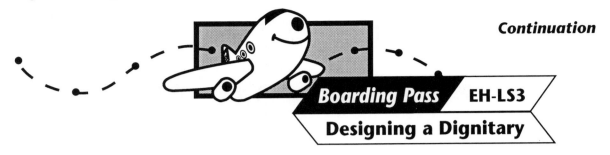

Boarding Pass | **EH-LS3**

Designing a Dignitary

Product Ideas for Presenting Your Dignitary

Make sure your products reflect your dignitary's outgoing personal and social behaviors or his or her sound foundation of social and moral values.

Level 1

- Design a report card for your dignitary when he or she was in the same grade that you are in now. What did the teacher have to say about your dignitary?
- Write a page from the diary of your dignitary in the first person.

Level 2

- Find some pictures to show your dignitary's favorite memories. Choose a childhood memory and write about it in the first person.
- Plan a vacation to another country for your dignitary. Write about something that happened on the trip.
- Fill out a job application for your dignitary. Write a letter from your dignitary to a friend, describing why this job would be perfect for your dignitary.
- Design a special award for your dignitary. What did she or he do to earn this special award? What was it for? Why is it important?

Level 3

- Your dignitary has written a letter to an advice columnist. What problem is facing your dignitary? Write the letter and the response from the columnist.
- Pretend you meet your dignitary. When, where, and how did you meet?
- What did you like about your dignitary? What did you dislike? Write a short play about this meeting. Have a friend play the part of your dignitary and act out your meeting.
- Write a news story about your dignitary. Give the story a headline and a photo. Describe the public reaction to the news story.
- Write a play in which your dignitary interacts with another person's dignitary. Perform the play for an audience.
- If your dignitary were given three wishes, what would he or she wish for? Why?

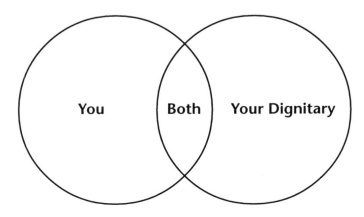

Ticket for Success

Flight # EH-LS4

Itinerary: Your Character is a Real Character

1. Authors develop a successful story by using writing strategies such as *characterization*, *dialogue*, *conflict*, and *plot development*. Write a story using the dignitary you developed in EH-LS3 "Designing a Dignitary."

2. As you develop the main character in your story, pay close attention to character types. See Boarding Pass EH-LS4 to discover important elements of character types that are found in interesting stories. Include at least one of each of these types of characters in your story.

3. Create a central conflict for your story. See Boarding Pass EH-LS4 for definitions of various types of conflict.

4. Make sure that your plot is developed into separate incidents. Most plots are broken down into a five-part plot structure. Boarding Pass EH-LS4 defines five types of conflict commonly used in writing.

5. Develop dialogue between your characters, but make sure that the reader knows who is speaking. Also, make sure that you give your character a "voice," by thinking of the unique qualities of your character and trying to match his or her words to that unique personality.

6. Peer edit your story with an adult or friend.

7. When you have completed your story, illustrate it and submit it for publishing if it is one of your best works. Boarding Pass EH-LA9 lists various publishers.

Departure Date: _____ **ETA:** _____
Mileage Perks: *Up to ★2,000 Frequent-Flyer Miles★*
Destination Skills: *creative and critical thinking, problem solving, communication*
Boarding During: *Language Arts*

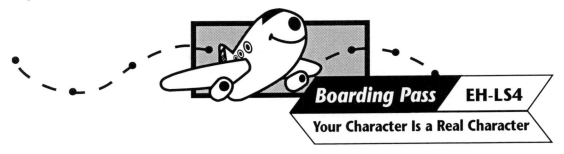

Boarding Pass / **EH-LS4**
Your Character Is a Real Character

Types of characters: Develop each of the following character types in your story. Your main character may fit the definition for several of the character types.

- *round character:* well developed; has many complex personality traits, demonstrated in a variety of ways
- *flat character:* not well developed; one or two key traits
- *dynamic (changing) character:* undergoes significant change from the beginning to the end of the story
- *static character:* does not changes over the course of the story
- *stock character:* stereotype (blonde, mad scientist, jock, sidekick, prince charming, perfect child, and so on)
- *character foil:* an extreme opposite to the main character; highlighting the main character's personality and actions by placing the opposite next to him or her
- *protagonist:* the central character who is trying to accomplish something
- *antagonist:* the force opposing the protagonist

Conflicts: Conflict is the clash of opposing forces and is a vital part of most plots. Five types of conflict are defined below. Make sure that your story includes at least one of these types of conflict.

- *character vs. character:* a character faces a problem with other characters
- *character vs. self:* a character faces a physical or emotional problem or struggle
- *character vs. society:* a character faces a problem with a group or part of society (government, schools, the law, and so on)
- *character vs. nature:* a character faces a problem with some force of nature (cold, storm, wildlife, and so on)
- *character vs. supernatural:* a character faces a problem with a force such as fate, luck, and so on

Plot development: Most story plots can be broken down into a traditional five-part plot structure. Your story should follow this development.

- *exposition:* an introduction to the main characters, settings, and rising situations of the plot
- *rising action:* the events and complications that lead to an important and dramatic point in the plot
- *climax:* the point of greatest interest and emotional involvement in the plot
- *falling action:* the events that develop from the climax and lead to the conclusion
- *resolution:* the final outcome, which ties up any loose ends left in the story

Who are the main characters in your story? What are the character types of each of your characters?

_____

What type of conflict is found in your story? Give a brief overview of the conflict that occurs in your story.

_____

What is the climax of your story? What events lead to this dramatic point? What is the outcome?

_____

Passport to Learn ©2001 Zephyr Press, Tucson, Arizona • 800-232-2187 • www.zephyrpress.com

Ticket for Success

Flight # EH-LS5

Honorable Mention

The National Honor Society was established to recognize outstanding high school students. Students who are nominated to the National Honor Society have demonstrated excellence in *scholarship*, *leadership*, *service*, and *character*. Many school systems also have a National Junior Honor Society to recognize outstanding students at the middle school level.

1. Read more about the National Honor Society on Boarding Pass EH-LS5.

2. Design your own Honor Society that recognizes the students who are outstanding in other areas, perhaps the arts (music, drama, and visual arts).

3. What name would you use for your new Honor Society? What would be the entry requirements and the membership rules for your new society?

4. Design a logo that would be used on the pin, certificate, and program cover for your new Honor Society. Design a program for an induction (joining) ceremony to honor your new members. Write a pledge for your Honor Society members to recite.

5. Extension: Propose your new Honor Society to the administration in your school system. Explain how it would honor outstanding students who are not normally publicly honored.

Departure Date: _____ **ETA:** _____
Mileage Perks: *Up to ★2,000 Frequent-Flyer Miles★*
Destination Skills: *critical thinking, higher-level thinking communication, leadership*
Boarding During: *Language Arts or Social Studies*

Boarding Pass / **EH-LS5**

Honorable Mention

The National Honor Society is more than just an honor roll. Rules for membership are based on the following:

- **Scholarship:** Students must have a cumulative grade point average of 85 percent, B, 3.0 (on a 4.0 scale) or equivalent standard of excellence, or a higher cumulative average, set by the local school's faculty.

- **Service:** Students must make voluntary contributions to the school or community, done without compensation and with a positive, courteous, and enthusiastic spirit.

- **Leadership:** Students must be resourceful, good problem solvers, promoters of school activities, idea-contributors, dependable, and persons who exemplify positive attitudes about life.

- **Character:** Students must uphold principles of morality and ethics; be cooperative, demonstrate high standards of honesty and reliability; show courtesy, concern, and respect for others; and maintain a good, clean lifestyle.

- **Citizenship:** Students must demonstrate citizenship, understand the importance of civic involvement, have a high regard for freedom, justice, and democracy, and demonstrate mature participation and responsibility through involvement with such activities as scouting, community organizations, and school clubs.

Induction Pledge:

I pledge myself to uphold the high purposes of the National Honor Society to which I have been selected; I will be true to the principles for which it stands; I will be loyal to my school, and encourage high standards of scholarship, service, leadership, and character.

For more information about the National Honor Society or National Junior Honor Society, contact the national office:

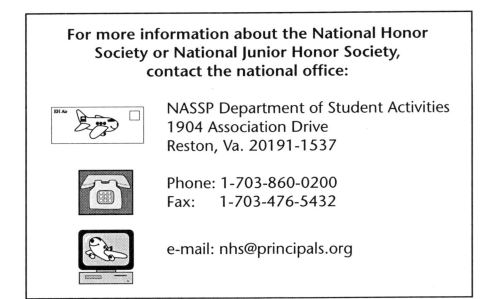

NASSP Department of Student Activities
1904 Association Drive
Reston, Va. 20191-1537

Phone: 1-703-860-0200
Fax: 1-703-476-5432

e-mail: nhs@principals.org

The National Honor Society and National Junior Honor Society along with their insignia and logos are the intellectual property of the National Association of Secondary School Principals (NASSP), duly protected, and used with permission of the association.

Ticket for Success

Flight # EH-LS6

Itinerary: One Shining Moment

Heroes use courage in many ways, such as:

- taking a risk to save a life
- giving up something for the good of others
- refusing to call it quits despite the odds
- accepting the challenge of what needs to be done

1. Look through newspapers, magazines, watch TV news shows, and surf the Internet to find a living person who is considered by many to be a hero.

2. Write an essay describing how you think your hero used several of the character attributes listed in Boarding Pass EH-LS6.

3. From your essay, write a speech telling your audience why this person is a true modern-day hero. Use at least three lifeskills as support.

4. Search for the address of this hero and write a letter or e-mail telling this special person why he or she is a hero to you. Congratulate this person on his or her efforts and express how much they mean to you.

Departure Date: _____ **ETA:** _____

Mileage Perks: *Up to ★2,000 Frequent-Flyer Miles★*

Destination Skills: *communication, critical thinking, inquiry, research*

Boarding During: *Language Arts or Social Studies*

Lifeskills

Adapted with permission from Kovalik, Susan, and Karen Olson. *ITI: The Model, Integrated Thematic Instruction.*

Citizenship: to behave as a supportive, contributing member of a country or community

Common sense: to use good judgment

Cooperation: to work together toward a common goal or purpose

Curiosity: to desire to learn or know about a full range of things

Decision making: to have strategies for making up one's mind and forming opinions

Effort: to try your hardest and work tirelessly

Flexibility: to have the ability to alter plans when necessary

Friendship: to make and keep a friend through mutual trust and caring

Initiative: to do something because it needs to be done

Integrity: to be honest, upright, and of sound moral principle and character

Kindness: to be gentle and thoughtful toward others

Loyalty: to be devoted and faithful to family, friends, and country

Motivation: to want to do something and to be willing to move into action

Organization: to plan, arrange, and implement actions in an orderly way

Patience: to wait calmly for someone or something

Peace: to be calm and serene, not quarrelsome or violent

Perseverance: to continue in spite of difficulties

Problem solving: to create or seek solutions in difficult situations

Reliability: to be trustworthy and dependable

Respect: to honor self, others, and the environment

Responsibility: to be accountable for one's own actions

Self-control: to have command over one's own actions and feelings

Sense of humor: to laugh and be playful without hurting others

Ticket for Success

Flight # EH-LS7

Itinerary: Flop, Drop—Then Roll!

Making mistakes is the way that humans grow and learn. Nobody likes to fail or to look "dumb" or silly. But mistakes and failure should not limit your expanding horizons. You will never be capable of doing something successfully if you don't take some leaps. More often, instead of laughing at your mistakes or failures, people will admire you for trying. You might be the most gifted person in the world, but unless you put your talents to work, you will never know.

1. Read about one of the very gifted people listed on Boarding Pass EH-LS7. These people had failures or made mistakes in their lives, but they are now known for their successes. You will find some information on the web, but it would be best to read a biography or autobiography about the person you choose.

2. Write a short one- to two-page essay on how this person was able to overcome his or her mistakes or failures.

3. Set goals for yourself. Write a list of fears, obstacles, failures, or mistakes that you can change into positive goals. Examples:

   • I will not take failures so hard. Instead, I will see them as opportunities to grow.

   • I will work on my self-esteem, to maintain my self-worth even when things don't work out perfectly.

4. Make a product to share these positive goals with others, such as a *Keys to Success* book, an *Overcoming Failures* calendar, *Student Success* posters, or get ideas from the Product Ideas list in your *Flight Log* (page 42).

Departure Date: _____ **ETA:** _____

Mileage Perks: *Up to ★2,000 Frequent-Flyer Miles★*

Destination Skills: *critical thinking, inquiry, higher-level thinking, leadership*

Boarding During: *Language Arts or Social Studies*

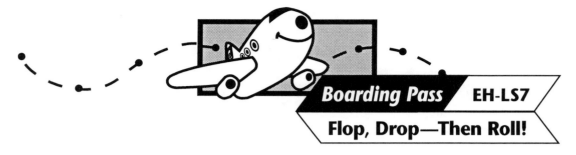

Boarding Pass / **EH-LS7**

Flop, Drop—Then Roll!

Gifted People Who Overcame Difficulties

Louisa May Alcott (author): told by an editor that she could never write anything that had popular appeal

Hans Christian Andersen (storyteller and writer): had difficulty reading, but was able to write

Winston Churchill (British prime minister): had much difficulty in school, failed sixth grade

Walt Disney (cartoonist and filmmaker): was slow in schoolwork, did not have a successful school experience; a newspaper editor fired him because he had "no good ideas"

Thomas Alva Edison (scientist and inventor): was unable to read until he was 12, wrote poorly throughout his life

Albert Einstein (physicist): did not speak until he was three; found schoolwork to be difficult, especially math, was thought to be "simple minded"

Thomas Jefferson (president): had many learning difficulties

Bruce Jenner (Olympic decathlon champ): barely got through school and was diagnosed as dyslexic; sports improved his self-esteem

Louis Pasteur (chemist and microbiologist): rated as "mediocre" in chemistry at Royal College

George Patton (general during WWII): could not read well; remained a poor reader throughout his life

Harriet Tubman (abolitionist): was struck in the head by an overseer as a child, fracturing her skull and resulting in narcolepsy for the rest of her life

George Washington (president): had difficulty spelling throughout his life; had very poor grammatical skills

Robin Williams (actor/comedian): has been diagnosed with ADHD

Henry Winkler (actor, director, producer): was called stupid and lazy as a child

Passport to Learn © 2001 Zephyr Press, Tucson, Arizona • 800-232-2187 • www.zephyrpress.com

Ticket for Success

Flight # EH-LS8

Itinerary: Reach Out

Becoming actively involved in community service helps young people to develop socially, emotionally, personally, and intellectually. It also has wonderful effects on one's self-esteem.

1. Organize a group of students to determine a community service project that will benefit members of your community. Some ideas are listed on Boarding Pass EH-LS8; however, feel free to come up with your own creative ideas.

2. Before you begin, do some research on how to effectively organize community service projects. *The Kid's Guide to Social Action* by Barbara Lewis is an excellent resource for ideas on how to get organized. An organization called Points of Light has many helpful resources as well. Information for obtaining these resources can be found on Boarding Pass EH-LS8.

3. Make sure you keep your parents, teacher, and principal informed of the plans that you are making.

4. Carry out your community service project during this school year.

5. Record the contributions you have made with pictures, thank-you cards, and volunteer statements. Create a poster or book.

Departure Date: _____ **ETA:** _____
Mileage Perks: *Up to ★★4,000 Frequent-Flyer Miles ★★*
Destination Skills: *communication, critical thinking, higher-level thinking, research, leadership*
Boarding During: *Language Arts or Social Studies*

Boarding Pass / EH-LS8

Reach Out

Volunteer and Community Service Ideas

"Adopt" one of the following:
- grandparent (help and visit elderly people in your community)
- historical building or monument (keep the area clean and plant flowers)
- homebound or disabled person (send cards or small gifts, visit, help)
- natural area (clean up a park, river, lake, road, and so on)
- primary-grade student (help a younger student feel more welcome at school; assist with school-work)
- school employee (a teacher's assistant, custodian, secretary, or one of your former teachers could probably use your help)

Clean school buses.

Clean the area around your school.

Conduct a food or coat drive.

Do bicycle repairs.

Do random acts of kindness whenever possible.

Encourage other young people to get involved in community service.

Help at a community service center or shelter.

Make holiday baskets and gifts to distribute to those in need in your community.

Make welcome baskets for new people in the community.

Organize a school staff appreciation day.

Paint over graffiti.

Participate in a walk-a-thon.

Plant flowers for a local school or church.

Sponsor one of the following:
- child in need from your own city
- child in need from another country
- pet at the humane society
- zoo animal

Work at the Special Olympics.

Excellent resources for organizing community service projects

The Kid's Guide to Social Action: How to Solve the Social Problems You Choose and Turn Creative Thinking into Positive Action by Barbara A. Lewis. 1991.

The Points of Light Foundation
1400 I Street, NW Suite 800
Washington, DC 20005
202-729-8000
Fax: 202-729-8100
e-mail: volnet@pointsoflight.org
http://www.pointsoflight.org

Ticket for Success

Flight # EH-LS9

Itinerary: Climbing the Career Ladder

1. Investigate a career that interests you using books, the Internet, and interviews with people who have chosen this career.

2. Write a three- to five-page report on your career choice. Include responses to some or all of the questions listed on Boarding Pass EH-LS9.

3. Think of yourself in the future, applying for a job in the career of your choice. Now that you know what qualifications a person should have for this profession, write a resume, cover letter, and business card as if you were applying for a job in this field. Research resume and cover letter writing on the website listed on Boarding Pass EH-LS9 or on other sites.

4. Showcase this career for your classmates by giving an informational report with graphics and props as well as by demonstrating a skill from your chosen career.

Departure Date: _____ **ETA:** _____

Mileage Perks: *Up to ★2,000 Frequent-Flyer Miles ★*

Destination Skills: *critical thinking, research, communication, leadership*

Boarding During: *Language Arts*

Boarding Pass / EH-LS9

Climbing the Career Ladder

Address some of the following questions in your career report:

- What is the history of this career or field?
- Will this career continue to be important in the future?
- How might this job change in the next five years? The next 10 years?
- What does a person in this career or field do each day?
- How are the basic skills of reading, writing, mathematics, listening, and speaking used in this career?
- Which of the following problem-solving skills are needed for this career, and how do they apply?
    organizing and planning
    interpreting and communicating information
    thinking creatively
    making decisions
    analyzing problems
- Which of the following "people" skills are needed for this career, and how are they used?
    serving customers
    participating as a team member
    teaching
    leading
    resolving conflict
- Which of the following self-management skills are needed, and how are they applied?
    setting short- and long-term goals
    evaluating one's own actions and accomplishments
    using constructive criticism
    using time efficiently and effectively
- How is technology used in this career?
- What kinds of personal traits, interests, and learning styles match this job?
- What does this career look like at the entry level?
- What advancements are possible for a person in this career?
- What is the basic education and training required for this career?
- What education or training is needed to advance in this field?
- What other jobs and careers are related to this field?
- What volunteer or work experience would help you learn more about this career?
- What studies, classes, degrees, and training should you be considering as you continue your education?
- What are the advantages of this career?
- What are the disadvantages of this career?
- What is the average yearly salary for this career?

For resume-writing tips, check the following website or use keywords: **resume writing**
    ▶ http://www.jobweb.org/catapult/guenov/restips.html

Ticket for Success

Flight # EH-LS10

Itinerary: Leave Them Speechless

Speeches are given for a variety of reasons, but mostly to inform, persuade, or entertain.

1. Write three different speeches.

   - To inform: Tell the PTA of your school about your school's program for high-potential students or about the *Tickets for Success* that you have worked on during the *Passport to Learn* program.

   - To persuade: Convince your school Board of Education that additional programs need to be offered for high-potential students in order to keep them interested, challenged, and to make the curriculum relevant to their lives.

   - To entertain: In a humorous way, explain to a group of teachers the joys and frustrations of the school experience for a high-potential student.

2. On boarding Pass EH-LS10 you will find helpful hints for giving speeches. Use these as you practice your speeches.

3. Present at least one of your speeches to the appropriate audience.

Departure Date: _____ **ETA:** _____

Mileage Perks: *Up to ★2,000 Frequent-Flyer Miles ★*

Destination Skills: *critical and creative thinking, communication, leadership*

Boarding During: *Language Arts or Social Studies*

Boarding Pass / EH-LS10

Leave Them Speechless

Giving Your Speech—Ten Helpful Hints

1. **Know what you want your speech to do.**
   - Informative speech describes something or states how to do something so the audience will understand and remember the information.
   - Persuasive speech causes the audience to change its beliefs or actions or to agree with what you believe.
   - Entertaining speech pleases, interests, and amuses the audience by using humor, puns, plays on words, anticlimax, and exaggeration.

2. **Stand confidently.**
   - Stand straight and alert.
   - Move as little as possible without appearing wooden. Use movement for a purpose.

3. **Match your expressions, gestures, and body language with what you are saying.**
   - Use facial expressions such as smiling, raising an eyebrow, smirking, frowning, grimacing, pouting, and grinning only when appropriate for your speech.
   - Use gestures such as thumbs up, head nodding and shaking, and shrugging only when appropriate for your speech.
   - Use body language such as turning away, stroking your chin, crossing your arms on your chest only when appropriate for your speech.

4. **Speak clearly.**
   - Speak loudly enough for everyone to hear.
   - Pronounce words distinctly.
   - Use a relaxed rate of speech. Avoid the natural tendency to speak quickly.

5. **Look at your audience.**
   - Smile and look confident.

6. **When making a major point, change your voice.**
   - Pitch: Strengthen or soften your voice for emphasis.
   - Volume: Raise or lower your voice to make a point.
   - Stress: Emphasize important words.

7. **Be prepared and practice.**
   - Know your content and your audience.
   - First practice by yourself, possibly in front of a mirror. Then practice in front of a family member or a friend.

8. **Focus on the purpose of your speech.**
   - Make note cards to help you stick to your topic.

9. **Add variety and interest with visual aids.**
   - Use interesting but simple overhead transparencies, PowerPoint® presentations, and props.

10. **Close with meaning and emotion.**
    - Think about how the audience will remember what you have said.
    - Leave time for questions from the audience.

For more information on giving effective speeches, contact:

Toastmasters International
P.O. Box 9052
Mission Viejo, CA 92690

949-858-8255

website: http://
www.toastmasters.org

Chapter 7

Expanding Horizons
Tickets for Success

Ticket for Success

Flight # EH-SS1

Itinerary: What's Up When You're Down?

1. Choose a country in the Southern Hemisphere that interests you (Australia, Brazil, New Zealand, South Africa, and so on).

2. List what you would like to know about how this country differs from ours, and develop at least five questions to investigate using the Internet, computer CDs, TV, books, encyclopedias, or other available sources. Examples will be found on Boarding Pass EH-SS1.

3. Research to find the answers to your questions through computer CDs, Internet, interviews, TV, books, and so on.

4. Use the Venn diagram on Boarding Pass EH-SS1 to compare and contrast the characteristics of the United States and the Southern Hemisphere country you chose.

5. Design a brochure promoting a vacation to the country you have researched, describing the out-of-this-world experiences available there.

6. Write a proposal to your parents to fund the money for a visit to your chosen location.

Departure Date: _____ **ETA:** _____

Mileage Perks: *Up to ★2,000 Frequent-Flyer Miles★*

Destination Skills: *creative thinking, inquiry, research, communication*

Boarding During: *Social Studies or Language Arts*

Passport to Learn ©2001 Zephyr Press, Tucson, Arizona • 800-232-2187 • www.zephyrpress.com

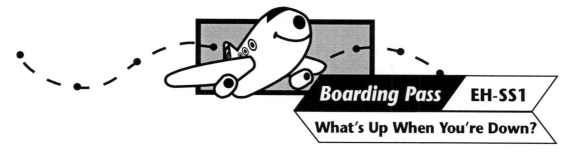

Boarding Pass / **EH-SS1**

What's Up When You're Down?

Choose a country in the Southern Hemisphere and write its name here.

_____

Here is a start on a list of questions that you might ask about a country in the Southern Hemisphere.

- Do their toilets flush clockwise or counterclockwise?
- What stars and constellations are visible only in the Southern Hemisphere?
- Do the phases of the moon (waxing and waning) differ in the two hemispheres?
- How does their compass compare with ours?

Add your own questions. Possibilities might include questions about food, music, leaders, and so on.

_____

_____

_____

_____

Compare and contrast characteristics of countries in the two hemispheres.

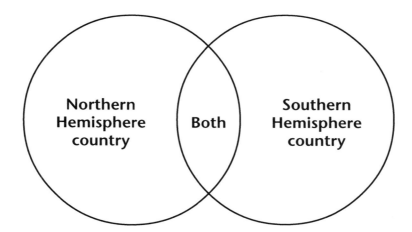

▶ Summarize how countries in the Northern Hemisphere are the same and different from countries in the Southern Hemisphere. How would the similarities and differences change your daily life if you lived there?

▶ Design a trifold brochure promoting a vacation to the location you have researched, describing the out-of-this-world experiences available there. See guidelines for creating a brochure on the continuation of Boarding Pass EH-SS1.

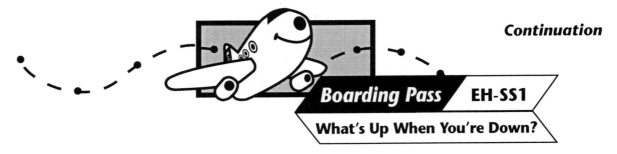

Boarding Pass / **EH-SS1**

What's Up When You're Down?

Guidelines for Producing a Travel Brochure

A travel brochure is an informative, educational, and persuasive device that must present information in a clear and organized manner. A travel brochure is not an in-depth study of a location, but it should give enough information about the location to grab and keep the reader's interest from start to finish. Because it doesn't tell the whole story about a location, it should contain the most important key points. Consider listing some information in simple bulleted lists or charts.

Steps to Creating a Memorable Travel Brochure

1. Write down what you currently know "off the top of your head" about your location. Describe your location. Write down key landmarks, interesting tourist spots, or historically significant locations that you now know about.
2. Go to a travel agency and collect sample brochures that appeal to you.
3. Identify those that have a style or format you might like to imitate or borrow. See how much detail each type of brochure includes.
4. Research your location. Use CD-ROMs, the Internet, interviews, videos, books, and so on. From these materials and what you already know about the topic, start picking out five to six significant or interesting facts that you think you will want to highlight in your brochure.
5. Write a catchy title, headlines, and subheads. Write the descriptive text. Group some information in lists and charts.
6. Sketch out some rough ideas of how you want your brochure to look—including any graphics you think you want to use. You might want to use clip art or, if you have access to a scanner, you may be able to scan artwork or your own graphics. Try out different formats to fit your text. Experiment.
7. Using the page layout software available to you, transfer your rough sketches to the computer. Your software may have templates or wizards that will provide you with even more ideas.
8. Print your final design and fold as necessary.

Questions to Ask about Your Final Design

- Does the brochure give enough information (including a map and directions) so the reader knows where to find the place and wants to visit it?
- Does the brochure tell what is significant (historical importance, tourist attractions, famous residents, significant industries, and so on) about this place?
- Are there interesting pictures? Pictures with people are usually more effective, but pictures of well-known landmarks or beautiful scenery can work without people in them.
- Are the graphics useful? Do they help to tell the story or do they seem to be just filling up space?

Ticket for Success

Flight # EH-SS2

Itinerary: Been There—Done That

1. Choose one of the 12 destination cities on your trip around the world.

2. Choose 12 natural objects or artifacts unique to that location, one from each category listed below (see Boarding Pass EH-SS2 for examples).

   - agricultural
   - architectural
   - arts
   - ecological
   - historical
   - monetary
   - natural
   - occupational
   - political
   - popular culture
   - religious
   - scenic

3. For each natural object or artifact, write a description and explain why you chose it to represent your location.

4. Once you have studied and described the 12 artifacts that actually exist in your location, now invent a new artifact that does not exist right now. This new artifact could represent a possible change that might occur during the third millennium in one of the 12 categories.

5. Finally, create a container (a box, bag, trunk, or so on) for any artifacts you have made or collected. This also should be representative of the culture or location.

Departure Date: _____ **ETA:** _____

Mileage Perks: *Up to ★2,000 Frequent-Flyer Miles★*

Destination Skills: *research, higher-level thinking*

Boarding During: *Social Studies or Language Arts*

Boarding Pass / **EH-SS2**

Been There—Done That

Natural Object: present in or produced by nature

Artifact: an object produced or shaped by human workmanship

The "Around the World Travel Destinations" include:

San Francisco, California   New Delhi, India   Reykjavík, Iceland
Honolulu, Hawaii   Cairo, Egypt   Halifax, Nova Scotia
Tokyo, Japan   Paris, France   New York, New York
Beijing, China   London, England   St. Louis, Missouri

Examples of Natural Objects and/or Artifacts from Honolulu, Hawaii

Natural: A volcano would be an excellent choice for Hawaii because the Hawaiian Islands are shield volcanoes (natural object).

Agricultural: As the pineapple is a well-established and highly exported crop from Hawaii, it is quite significant in the agricultural sector of Hawaii (natural object).

Architectural: The Iolani Palace is the palace of an ancient king. The Italian Renaissance architecture exemplifies Hawaiian use of varied architectural forms (artifact).

Your "Around-the-World Travel Destination" _____

Write an explanation of the artifact or natural object and why it was chosen to represent this location:

Scenic: _____

Natural: _____

Arts: _____

Historical: _____

Architectural: _____

Popular Culture: _____

Political: _____

Religious: _____

Agricultural: _____

Occupational: _____

Monetary: _____

Ecological: _____

Passport to Learn ©2001 Zephyr Press, Tucson, Arizona • 800-232-2187 • www.zephyrpress.com

Ticket for Success

Flight # EH-SS3

*Itinerary: Extraterrestrial Exploration

You are a scientist who studies alien populations and the structure of the societies in which they live. As part of your work, you are on a spaceship exploring the galaxy. You land on a planet and discover a native population.

1. What would you have to know about this extraterrestrial population to get a complete picture of how its society works? Do some research on the key characteristics of a society and a culture. You will need to create answers to questions like the following: What are the customs and beliefs of the population? If there is a form of government? If so, how does it work? What kind of monetary system is used? How are the young taught?

2. Report your findings in a booklet describing the extraterrestrial society.

3. Create an artifact that would be appropriate to the extraterrestrial population you have described. Make sure that the item truly reflects the society you have imagined.

4. Design a product which will persuade people from Earth to go and join the newly discovered population on a distant planet. Use you best persuasive techniques to describe the advantages of living there.

*There is no Boarding Pass for this ticket.

Departure Date: _____ **ETA:** _____

Mileage Perks: *Up to ★2,000 Frequent-Flyer Miles★*

Destination Skills: *creative thinking, research, higher-level thinking*

Boarding During: *Social Studies or Language Arts*

Ticket for Success

Flight # EH-SS4

Itinerary: Seven Up

Most people agree that the Seven Wonders of the Ancient World are the most amazing monuments built by humans in the ancient world. These wonders are listed on Boarding Pass EH-SS4.

1. Investigate the Seven Wonders of the Ancient World. Write a description of each wonder and a justification for why it is considered one of the Seven Wonders.

2. Even though lists exist for the Seven Wonders of the Modern World and the Seven Wonders of the Natural World, there is no agreed upon formal list as there is for the ancient world. Suggestions for places that might be on official lists for the Seven Wonders of the Modern World and Seven Wonders of the Natural World are found on Boarding Pass EH-SS4.

3. Investigate the possible Wonders of the Modern World, and the Natural World on Boarding Pass EH-SS4. Make lists of what you think should be named the "official" Seven Wonders of the Modern World and the Seven Wonders of the Natural World. Write a justification of why the wonders you have picked are the best so that others will agree with your opinion.

4. Submit your ideas to a publishing company that might put your suggestions in print. Refer to Boarding Pass EH-LA9 for a list of publishers.

Departure Date: _____ **ETA:** _____

Mileage Perks: *Up to ★2,000 Frequent-Flyer Miles★*

Destination Skills: *research, higher-level thinking*

Boarding During: *Social Studies or Language Arts*

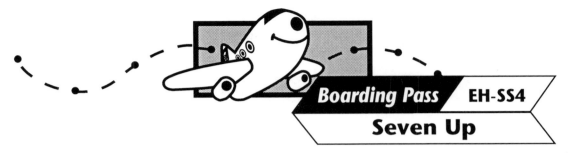

Boarding Pass / **EH-SS4**

Seven Up

Seven Wonders of the Ancient World

Since ancient times, people have put together lists of world wonders. Most people agree on the list of the Seven Wonders of the Ancient World.

1. The Pyramids of Egypt

2. The Hanging Gardens of Babylon (built by Nebuchadnezzar II)

3. The Temple of the Greek Goddess Artemis at Ephesus

4. The Statue of the Greek God Zeus at Olympia

5. The Marble Tomb of King Mausolus at Halicarnassus

6. The Colossus of Rhodes (Statue of Greek God Helios) in the Aegean Sea

7. The Pharos (Lighthouse) at Alexandria, Egypt

The three websites listed below will be helpful as you investigate these wonders or use keywords: **Wonders of the World**

▶ http://unmuseum.mus.pa.us/wonders.htm

▶ http://cnn.com/TRAVEL/DESTINATIONS/9705/seven.wonders/

▶ http://ce.eng.usf.edu/pharos/wonders/

Another excellent resource is:

▶ *The World Almanac and Book of Facts*

Boarding Pass / **EH-SS4**

Seven Up

Modern and Natural Wonders

Formal lists do not exist for the Seven Wonders of the Modern World or the Seven Wonders of the Natural World. However, several suggestions have been made for these lists. Which wonders would be your pick?

Suggestions for Wonders of the Modern World

1. The Suez Canal in Egypt
2. The Eiffel Tower in Paris, France
3. The Alaska Highway
4. The Golden Gate Bridge in San Francisco
5. The Empire State Building in New York
6. Dneproges Dam, Dnieper River, Ukraine
7. The Panama Canal, Panama
8. The Channel Tunnel between France and England
9. The Clock Tower (Big Ben) in London, England
10. The CN Tower in Toronto, Canada
11. The Gateway Arch in St. Louis, Missouri
12. The High Dam in Aswan, Egypt
13. Hoover Dam in Arizona/Nevada
14. Itaipú Dam in Brazil/Paraguay
15. Mount Rushmore National Memorial in South Dakota
16. The Petronas Towers in Kuala Lumpur, Malaysia
17. The Statue of Cristo Redentor in Rio de Janeiro, Brazil
18. The Statue of Liberty in New York City
19. The Sydney Opera House in Australia
20. The Taj Mahal in Agra, North India
21. The Easter Island Statues in Chile
22. The Great Wall of China
23. The Space Shuttle, USA
24. Chartres Cathedral in France
25. Netherlands North Sea Protection Works

Suggestions for Wonders of the Natural World

1. Mount Everest in Nepal
2. Victoria Falls, Zambia/Zimbabwe
3. The Grand Canyon in Arizona
4. The Great Barrier Reef in Australia
5. The Northern Lights (Aurora Borealis)
6. Paricutin (a 1943-born Mexican volcano)
7. The Harbor at Rio de Janeiro, Brazil
8. Angel Falls in Venezuela
9. The Bay of Fundy in Nova Scotia, Canada
10. Iguassu Falls in Brazil/Argentina
11. Krakatoa Volcano in Indonesia
12. Mount Fuji in Japan
13. Mount Kilimanjaro in Tanzania
14. Niagara Falls in Ontario (Canada) and New York State
15. Yellowstone National Park in Wyoming
16. Old Faithful in Wyoming
17. The Petrified Forest in Arizona
18. The Redwoods in California
19. The Amazon River in South America
20. The Badlands in South Dakota
21. The Rainforest in Brazil
22. Geothermal features of Iceland and Greenland

Passport to Learn © 2001 Zephyr Press, Tucson, Arizona • 800-232-2187 • www.zephyrpress.com

Ticket for Success

Flight # EH-SS5

Itinerary: One Moment in Time

1. Read about the history of time capsules on Boarding Pass EH-SS5.

2. Generate a list of things you would place in a time capsule for the beginning of the third millennium and another list of what you predict might be placed in a time capsule for the beginning of the fourth millennium.

3. What would you use to make your time capsule canister? Keep in mind the ideas and cautions listed on Boarding Pass EH-SS5. Write a one-page explanation of how you will make your time capsule.

4. Make a time capsule containing 10 to 15 actual objects that you think would be important to preserve today so that people of the future will understand this moment in time.

5. How will you make sure people of the future will know where they should go to dig up your capsule? In a one-page paper, write your directions for finding and opening your time capsule 100 years from now. Include how and where you will record the location of your time capsule.

Departure Date: _____ **ETA:** _____

Mileage Perks: *Up to ★2,000 Frequent-Flyer Miles★*

Destination Skills: *creative and critical thinking, research, higher-level thinking*

Boarding During: *Social Studies or Language Arts*

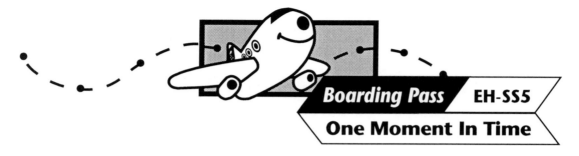

Boarding Pass / EH-SS5
One Moment In Time

History: What Is a Time Capsule?

A time capsule is usually a sturdy container that can withstand the effects of time and the elements. The Egyptians were famous users of historical time capsules, building pyramids to honor people and hold objects for the afterlife. They also preserved for the future clues about Egyptian life.

In 1939, Westinghouse Electric created a time capsule for the World's Fair and put the following contents inside: alarm clock, can opener, eyeglasses, fountain pen, electric lamp, miniature camera, nail file, safety pin, slide rule, toothbrush, watch, Mickey Mouse cup, Sears Roebuck catalog, cigarettes, baseball, deck of cards, dollar bill, seeds, and a Holy Bible.

A second time capsule was created for the 1964 World's Fair. Many dramatic technological and social changes had occurred since 1939. This time the contents included a plastic heart valve, transistor radio, contact lenses, ballpoint pen, rechargeable flashlight, Polaroid camera, freeze-dried food, birth control pills, computer memory unit, watch, Beatles record, bikini, filtered cigarettes, tranquilizers, antibiotics, credit card, irradiated seeds, and a fifty-star American flag.

Time Capsule Construction Tips

The Container

Do . . .

- Select a container that is strong and waterproof and seal it in a waterproof bag.
- Ideally use copper, aluminum, or stainless steel for your container.
- Use metals that are seamless or welded.
- Seal the container with a screw-on cap or use an epoxy glue.

Do not . . .

- Use PVC pipe for time capsules. It will harm the environment.

The Contents

Do . . .

- Add a hard copy of any material on computer disks and identify the computer type.
- Include black-and-white properly processed photographic prints. Color prints may fade.
- Make photocopies of newsprint, since newsprint is acidic and deteriorates easily.
- Seal wooden objects in polyurethane bags. Keep wood away from electronic equipment.
- Use fibers that age well such as cotton and polyester.
- Put silica gel, sold in granulated form in art and hardware stores, into the container to absorb moisture.

Do not . . .

- Include videotapes or audiotapes because the equipment to play them back may not be available when the capsule is opened. Also, they deteriorate easily.
- Include rubber objects since rubber deteriorates and releases sulfur.
- Use silk, wool, nylon, or hair that may deteriorate and corrode metal.

Boarding Pass / **EH-SS5**

One Moment In Time

Time Capsule Construction Tips *(continued)*

The Location

Do . . .

- Place the capsule in a dry location.
- Place facing north if setting in a cornerstone.
- Include a list inside the capsule of the color and material of every object.
- Place at least three feet below the ground, if burying.
- Register your time capsule with the International Time Capsule Society. See below.

Do not . . .

- Put the capsule in a place where there are extreme temperature fluctuations or vibrations.

For additional information on time capsules, check the following references:

International Time Capsule Society (ITCS)
c/o Oglethorpe University
4484 Peachtree Road
Atlanta, GA 30319-2797
404-261-1441
Fax: 404-364-8500
www.oglethorpe.edu/itcs/

A detailed pamphlet on time capsules,
CCI Notes 1/6, is available from:
Canadian Conservation Institute
1030 Innes Road
Ottawa, Ont. K1A 0M8
Canada
613-998-3724
Fax: 613-998-4721

A series of pamphlets and publications on time capsules, suggestions for contents, and their preservation is available from:
Future Packaging
19834 Squire Drive
Covina, CA 91724-3457
818-966-1955

Tom Marak
Time Capsules, Inc.
107 Bauder School Road
Prospect, PA 16052
1-800-527-7853
e-mail: capsules@mrdigital.com

Ticket for Success

Flight # EH-SS6

*Itinerary: Kids Are People Too!

1. Imagine that the state legislature is considering changes to your state constitution. An advocacy group is proposing a Bill of Rights for Children and wishes you and your classmates to suggest items to be included. You will propose items for the Bill of Rights and include reasons why these rights are needed.

2. Research the Bill of Rights using books, the Internet, and CD-ROMs to see how it is written and what rights American citizens now have.

3. Brainstorm a list of at least five possible rights for children that should be included in your state Bill of Rights.

4. Write down reasons that will convince adults that children need these rights.

5. Present your proposed items and reasons to the class and see if they agree that these rights should be included.

6. Send your proposal to government representatives.

*There is no Boarding Pass for this ticket.

Departure Date: _____ **ETA:** _____
Mileage Perks: *Up to ★2,000 Frequent-Flyer Miles★*
Destination Skills: *creative and critical thinking, research, higher-level thinking*
Boarding During: *Social Studies or Language Arts*

Passport to Learn © 2001 Zephyr Press, Tucson, Arizona • 800-232-2187 • www.zephyrpress.com

Ticket for Success

Flight # EH-SS7

Itinerary: Cast Your Vote

1. Research the issues and platforms of the Democratic and Republican political parties. You can contact the national committee for each of the parties by using the resources listed on Boarding Pass EH-SS7.

2. Propose that a new party be formed. Over the years, there have been many third parties in the United States. None of them has won a national presidential election. Political parties can usually be classified into five different types, which are listed on Boarding Pass EH-SS7.

3. What type of party will you propose?

   - Name your party.

   - Develop a symbol, such as an elephant or a donkey for your party. Make sure you can explain why you chose that symbol.

   - Explain at least five major issues about which your party feels strongly and how your party stands on these issues. How do these positions differ from those of the Democratic and Republican parties?

   - Decide on the candidates you would support for president and vice-president in the next election.

   - Develop a campaign slogan.

4. Develop a portfolio or scrapbook to explain your party to the voters.

Departure Date: _____ **ETA:** _____

Mileage Perks: *Up to ★2,000 Frequent-Flyer Miles★*

Destination Skills: *creative and critical thinking, research*

Boarding During: *Social Studies or Language Arts*

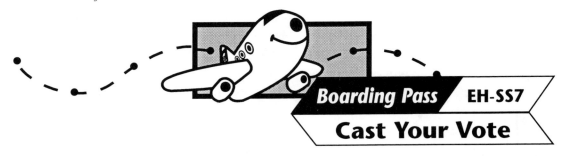

Boarding Pass / **EH-SS7**

Cast Your Vote

Third Parties: Five Different Types

1. Groups that broke away from the two major parties
   Examples: Liberal Republicans, 1872; Gold Democrats, 1856; American Independent Party, 1968

2. Organizations formed to help a specific group of people
   Examples: Greenback Party, 1870s (formed to promote currency expansion); Populist Party, 1890s (formed to help farmers who suffered from declining agricultural prices)

3. Left-wing protest groups
   Examples: Socialist Party, 1901; American Communist Party, 1919

4. Parties that have only one goal
   Example: Prohibition Party, 1869 (to prevent the manufacture and sale of alcoholic beverages in the United States)

5. Groups that have broad programs and try to gain national favor
   Examples: Progressive Parties, 1924, 1948, 1952; Libertarian Party, 1971; Reform Party, 1992; Green Party, 1984

Contact the national committees of the Democratic and Republican parties to find out where they stand on important political issues:

The Democratic Party

Democratic National Committee
430 S. Capitol St. SE
Washington, DC 20003
202-863-8000
www.democrats.org/contact/index.html
There is a guestbook on the site for e-mail.

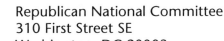

The Republican Party

Republican National Committee
310 First Street SE
Washington, DC 20003
202-863-8500
Fax: 202-863-8820
www.rnc.org
e-mail: info@rnc.org

Passport to Learn © 2001 Zephyr Press, Tucson, Arizona • 800-232-2187 • www.zephyrpress.com

Itinerary: Joust Do It!

The Earl of Essex in England, recently died. His will has been read and he has no known heirs. The castle that was in his family is now empty. His will states that the person who converts the castle into the best living museum, bringing the Middle Ages to life, will inherit the castle. The earl's estate is sponsoring a contest seeking the most authentic floor plan of a castle, including a redesign of the Grand Hall. The winner gets the castle!

1. Research castles to discover the most important features that should be included in a castle floor plan and in a model of a grand hall. Design a floor plan for the entire castle.

2. Rules for entry state that a diorama or model of the new Grand Hall in the Living Museum Castle must be submitted along with plans for the rest of the castle.

3. A banner, including the coat of arms representing the winner's family, will hang in the Grand Hall and must be depicted in the diorama or model. Investigate heraldry to assist you in designing the banner and coat of arms. Key facts on heraldry are found on Boarding Pass EH-SS8.

4. Design flyers for activities and special exhibits that will take place in the museum.

Departure Date: _____ **ETA:** _____

Mileage Perks: *Up to* ★★★ *6,000 Frequent-Flyer Miles* ★★★

Destination Skills: *creative thinking, research, higher-level thinking*

Boarding During: *Social Studies or Language Arts*

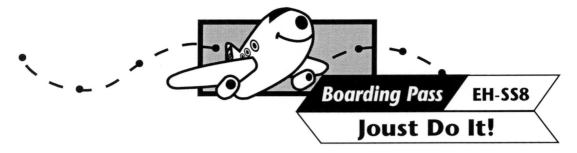

Boarding Pass / EH-SS8

Joust Do It!

An official coat of arms consists of several parts:

motto: a phrase representing the family
crest: an emblem that appears above the shield
shield elements: what appears on the shield (or escutcheon), their placement, and their colors
supporters: usually two animals, birds, or persons appearing on either side of the shield

Other unofficial considerations in the design of your coat of arms include:

motto design: the placement, banner, and typestyle are at the artist's discretion
wreath: a rope with six parts, using two of the official colors
helmet or helm: the helmet varied with rank, the century represented, and the artist's preference
shield shape: the shape changed throughout the centuries
mantle: represented the cloth that hung from the wreath and protected the back of the head and neck; looks somewhat like the leaves of a plant

Every element on the shield is important in the study of heraldry. Even the colors can have special meaning in a family crest or coat of arms:

Color	Heraldry term	Meaning
Gold	Or	generosity and elevation of the mind
Silver or White	Argent	peace and sincerity
Red	Gules	warrior or martyr: military strength
Blue	Azure	truth and loyalty
Green	Vert	hope, joy, and loyalty in love
Black	Sable	constancy or grief
Purple	Purpure	royal majesty, sovereignty, and justice
Orange	Tawny or Tenne	worthy ambition
Maroon	Sanguine or Murray	patience in battle, and ultimately victorious

For a wonderful listing of the special meanings of all of the symbols of heraldry, check this website or use keyword: **heraldry**

▶ http://fleurdelis.com

In the Table of Contents on this website, check under: "Is there a meaning behind symbols on coats of arms and crests?"

Passport to Learn © 2001 Zephyr Press, Tucson, Arizona • 800-232-2187 • www.zephyrpress.com

Ticket for Success

Flight # EH-SS9

Itinerary: Kid Biz

1. Learn about the free-enterprise system by investigating what it would take to start your own business.

2. Develop a business plan that would address the questions about starting a business on Boarding Pass EH-SS9 .

3. Develop forms needed for starting a business. A list of important forms you might need is listed on Boarding Pass EH-SS9.

4. Develop an advertising plan for your business.

5. Extension: Consider opening your business in your neighborhood during the summer. Present your business plan to your parents to see if they would approve of your business and support it.

6. Extension: Consider donating any profits your business makes to a worthy charity. Research a charity that fits with your beliefs.

Departure Date: _____ **ETA:** _____
Mileage Perks: *Up to ★ 2,000 Frequent-Flyer Miles ★*
Destination Skills: *creative and critical thinking, research*
Boarding During: *Social Studies, Language Arts, or Mathematics*

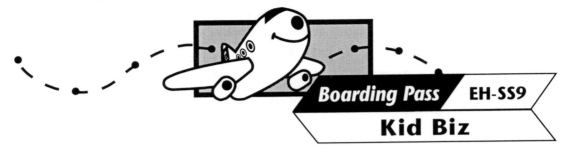

Boarding Pass **EH-SS9**

Kid Biz

Points to Address in Your Business Plan

What type of business will you start?

- Will you manufacture or produce a product to sell? Example: a lemonade stand
- Will you provide a service? Example: a lawn-mowing service

Justify that this is something consumers will want or need.

Estimate how much income your business will generate.

What will be the name of your business?

Where will your business be located?

How do you know that you can use this location for your business?

What will your business location look like?

What equipment will you need and where will you get it?

What supplies will you need and where will you get them?

What quantity of supplies will you need?

How will you get the money to purchase your supplies or rent your equipment?

How much will you charge for your product or service?

How will you repay any debts?

What will you do with your profit?

How long will you keep your business open?

Forms to Produce

Use the computer so that you produce a quality product (check office supply stores for samples of these types of forms).

- form to record all expenses and income
- loan application and agreement form.
- bills and receipts for customers when they buy your product or service

Advertising Plan for Your Business

Decide what type of advertising would work best for your business.

- flyers
- hats
- live commercials
- newspaper ads
- engraved pens or pencils
- posters
- T-shirts

Decide what information to include on your advertising materials.

Create your advertisements.

Post, distribute, or perform your advertisements.

Ticket for Success

Flight # EH-SS10

Itinerary: On a Revolutionary Note

If you want to learn facts about the conflicts of war, look in any textbook. But if you want to understand thoughts and emotions of the people involved, look to the songs of the time.

1. Make a list of the wars in which Americans have been involved since the Revolutionary War.

2. Many songs were used to encourage soldiers, to inspire public support, to praise the home country, or to promote negative ideas about an enemy. Unpopular wars such as the Vietnam War produced protest songs. Make your own list of wartime songs that were popular during these wars. Some are already listed for you on Boarding Pass EH-SS10.

3. Find the lyrics to these songs. Write a report on popular songs of American wars and study the lyrics to help others understand the thoughts and emotions of Americans during these times. Start your report by investigating at least 10 of the songs listed on Boarding Pass EH-SS10.

4. Compose your own song about your thoughts and emotions on the conflict of war.

Departure Date: _____ **ETA:** _____
Mileage Perks: *Up to ★ 2,000 Frequent-Flyer Miles ★*
Destination Skills: *creative thinking, research, higher-level thinking*
Boarding During: *Social Studies or Language Arts*

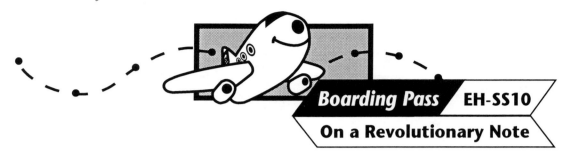

Boarding Pass / **EH-SS10**

On a Revolutionary Note

American Popular Music During Times of War

Yankee Doodle, Revolutionary War
Battle Hymn of the Republic, Civil War
Dixie, Civil War
John Brown's Body, Civil War
When Johnny Comes Marching Home, Civil War
Yellow Rose of Texas, Civil War
If You Were the Only Girl in the World, World War I
How Ya Gonna Keep 'Em Down on the Farm (After They've Seen Paree), World War I
Over There, World War I
Yankee Doodle Dandy, World War I
Boogie Woogie Bugle Boy, World War II
God Bless America, World War II
The Ballad of the Green Berets, Vietnam War
Blowin' in the Wind, Vietnam War
Who Will Answer, Vietnam War
We Gotta Get Out of This Place, Vietnam War
Turn, Turn, Turn, Vietnam War
Leaving on a Jet Plane, Vietnam War
Five Hundred Miles, Vietnam War
Where Have All the Flowers Gone? Vietnam War
God Bless the U.S.A. Gulf War

Other Patriotic Music

America the Beautiful
From the Halls of Montezuma
Grand Ole Flag
My Country 'Tis of Thee
Stars and Stripes Forever
The Star Spangled Banner
This Land Is Your Land
When the Saints Go Marching In

An excellent resource is:
► *The Green Book of Songs,* by Jeff Green

Chapter 8

Expanding Horizons
Tickets for Success

Mathematics

Ticket for Success

Flight # EH-M1

Itinerary: **Sum-Body Famous**

1. We often think of mathematicians as geniuses surrounded by the world of numbers. You may first think of a man with glasses and wild hair, writing numbers madly on a chalkboard. But famous mathematicians are creative men and women who often lead intellectually exciting lives. We need new mathematicians in the world today to continue the work of famous mathematicians of the past and invent solutions to new problems. Make a presentation to show people that the field of mathematics is a fine and fascinating area of study.

2. Use the Internet and other sources to research a famous mathematician. A list of suggestions is found on Boarding Pass EH-M1.

3. Discover your chosen mathematician's major contribution to the field of mathematics. Try to find out what life events led to your mathematician's significant accomplishments by including interesting details from his or her personal background and upbringing.

4. Write a three- to five-page report about your famous mathematician.

5. Present your research creatively to the class. Make a poster, write a play, produce a game show, make a video, or create a board game to present your findings in a memorable way.

Departure Date: _____ **ETA:** _____
Mileage Perks: *Up to ★2,000 Frequent-Flyer Miles★*
Destination Skills: *research, communication, critical thinking,*
Boarding During: *Mathematics or Language Arts*

Passport to Learn ©2001 Zephyr Press, Tucson, Arizona • 800-232-2187 • www.zephyrpress.com

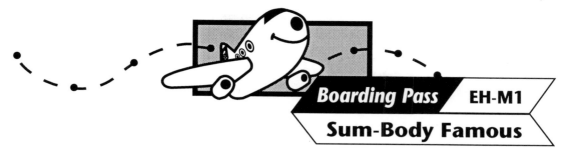

Boarding Pass **EH-M1**
Sum-Body Famous

Famous Mathematicians

This is an incomplete list of famous mathematicians. Choose from this list or choose another famous mathematician to study.

Pythagoras, 582–507 B.C.

Euclid, 300 B.C.

Archimedes, 287–212 B.C.

Caudius Ptolemy, A.D. 85–165

Hypatia, A.D. 370–415

Al-Khwarizmi, A.D. 783–840

Fibonacci, A.D. 1170–1250

Nicolaus Copernicus, A.D. 1473–1543

Girolamo Cardano, A.D. 1501–1576

John Napier, A.D. 1550–1617

Galileo Galilei, A.D. 1564–1642

Johannes Kepler, A.D. 1571–1630

René Descartes, A.D 1596–1650

Pierre de Fermat, A.D. 1601–1665

Blaise Pascal, A.D. 1623–1662

Sir Isaac Newton, A.D. 1642–1726

Gottfried Wilhelm Leibniz, A.D. 1646–1716

Johann Bernoulli, A.D. 1667–1748

Leonhard Euler, A.D. 1707–1783

Benjamin Banneker, A.D. 1731–1806

Pierre-Simon Laplace, A.D. 1749–1827

Sophie Germain, A.D. 1776–1806

Carl Friedrich Gauss, A.D. 1777–1855

Mary Fairfax Somerville, A.D. 1780–1872

Charles Babbage, A.D. 1791–1871

Ada Lovelace, A.D. 1815–1852

Sir Arthur Cayley, A.D. 1821–1895

Sonya Kovalevskaya, A.D. 1850–1891

Jules-Henri Poincaré, A.D. 1854–1912

Albert Einstein, A.D. 1879–1955

Two of the best websites giving the most complete information are:

Women in Mathematics:
► www.agnesscott.edu/lriddle/women/women.htm

Biographies of Mathematicians:
► www-history.mcs.st-and.ac.uk/history/biogindex.html

Itinerary: Align a Design

A fractal is a geometric construction that is self-similar at different scales. In other words, a fractal shape will look the same no matter at what size it is viewed.

1. Using a search engine such as Yahoo or Altavista, search for a *Sierpinski triangle*. A Sierpinski triangle is a fine example of a fractal, since you can zoom in to any of the sub-triangles and it will look exactly like the entire Sierpinski triangle itself.

2. Construct a Sierpinski triangle using the directions on Boarding Pass EH-M2.

3. Extension: Continue learning about fractals by doing research on the Von Koch snowflake. Using the directions you find on the website (http://math.rice.edu/~lanius/frac/koch.html), construct a Von Koch snowflake.

4. Using a fractal design, construct something colorful and creative that could be used in the real world. Examples are a flag for the holes on a golf course, a T-shirt for your class, and so on.

Departure Date: _____ **ETA:** _____

Mileage Perks: *Up to ★2,000 Frequent-Flyer Miles★*

Destination Skills: *research, critical and creative thinking*

Boarding During: *Mathematics or Art*

Boarding Pass / **EH-M2**

Align a Design

Constructing a Famous Fractal— a Sierpinski Triangle

1. Construct an equilateral triangle (a triangle having equal sides as shown in figure 1). It would be best to make this triangle large, with each side measuring eight inches.

2. Connect the midpoints of each side, forming four equilateral triangles. Shade the triangle in the center, as shown in figure 2.

3. Now, perform the step-two process on each of the three unshaded equilateral triangles. figure 3 shows this procedure being done to one of the three smaller triangles. Make sure you shade the center triangle as in step 2.

4. Follow the same procedure for the nine smaller triangles.

Figure 1

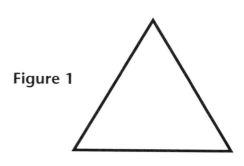

Figure 2

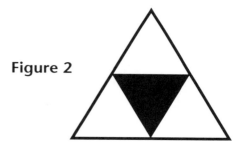

Figure 3

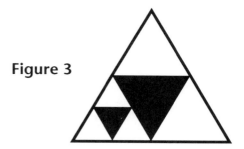

An excellent website for the Sierpinski triangle is:

▶ http://math.rice.edu/~lanius/fractals/sierjava.html

Also use keywords: **fractal, Sierpinski triangle, or Von Koch snowflake**

Ticket for Success

Flight # EH-M3

Itinerary: And the First Shall Be Last

If palindromes fascinated you in EH-LA1 (page 48), you will find a challenge in working on three-digit number palindromes (100–999).

1. Study the chart on Boarding Pass EH-M3 which shows the frequency of the number of reversals needed to make three-digit numbers into palindromes. For instance, there are 90 numbers between 100 and 999 that take zero reversals to become a palindrome (for example: 101, 555, 898, and so on). There are 213 numbers between 100 and 999 that take one reversal to become a palindrome (for example: 100 + 001 = 101, 102 + 201 = 303, and so on).

2. Make a chart similar to the one shown below and discover the palindromes for the three-digit numbers. You'll become an addition expert!

Three-digit numbers	Number of reversals	Palindrome produced
100	1	101
101	0	101
102	1	303
103	1	404
104	1	505
105	1	606
etc.		

Departure Date: _____ **ETA:** _____

Mileage Perks: *Up to ★2,000 Frequent-Flyer Miles★*

Destination Skills: *problem solving*

Boarding During: *Mathematics*

Passport to Learn © 2001 Zephyr Press, Tucson, Arizona • 800-232-2187 • www.zephyrpress.com

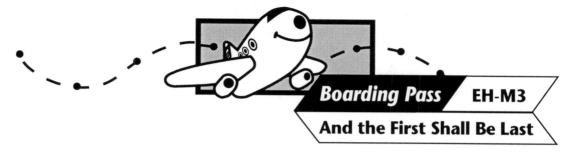

Boarding Pass / **EH-M3**

And the First Shall Be Last

3-Digit Palindromes

Conjecture: There exist 3-digit positive integers which do not produce a palindromic sum.

Number	Number of reversals	Palindrome produced
100	1	101
251	2	707
252	0	252
253	2	1,111
276	15	8,836,886,388

Palindromes—3-Digit Numbers

Number of reversals	Frequency
0	90
1	213
2	281
3	145
4	63
5	31
6	9
7	17
8	7
9	0
10	2
11	7
12	0
13	0
14	2
15	7
16	0
17	4
18	0
19	0
20	0
21	0
22	2
23	7
>23	13

Ticket for Success

Flight # EH-M4

Itinerary: Culinary Travels

You can learn a great deal about countries and cultures by studying the foods and recipes that come from different places.

1. Study foods and recipes from your destination countries and locations. Hawaii, Japan, China, India, France, and England have many special foods and recipes that originated in these places. Iceland does not have many dishes that can be called specifically Icelandic in origin. Most of the recipes used in Iceland have been adapted from other cuisines, most noticeably from that of their Danish forefathers. Egyptian foods reflect the country's melting-pot history. Native cooks using local ingredients have modified Greek, Turkish, Lebanese, Palestinian, and Syrian traditions. Your destinations in North America use recipes from around the globe, although Missouri features Amish and Ozark recipes and California specializes in vegetarian delights. New York has its cheesecake, New England its clam chowder, and Nova Scotia prides itself on its seafood.

2. Create a World Destination Cookbook with a least one recipe from each country on your journey. Make your cookbook colorful, adding pictures of the dishes you choose.

3. As a tasty finalé, prepare and serve your class one of your culinary delights.

4. Extension: Research the differences between the measurement systems used for cooking in different countries. In the U.S., we measure many ingredients by volume in cups but also with Imperial weights and measures. In other parts of the world, you will find ingredients measured using the metric system. Boarding Pass EH-M4 will get you started. If you try to cook with recipes you have converted, remember the golden rule—stick to one form of measurement throughout a recipe; don't mix cups of flour with grams of butter.

Departure Date: _____ **ETA:** _____
Mileage Perks: *Up to ★2,000 Frequent-Flyer Miles★*
Destination Skills: *research, problem solving, creative thinking*
Boarding During: *Mathematics, Language Arts, Reading, or Social Studies*

Boarding Pass / **EH-M4**

Culinary Travels

Weight and Oven Temperature Conversion Tables

Weight Conversions	
Ounces/Pounds	**Metric**
1/2 oz.	14 g
1 oz.	28 g
2 oz.	57 g
3 oz.	85 g
4 oz. (1/4 lb.)	113 g
5 oz.	142 g
6 oz.	170 g
7 oz.	198 g
8 oz. (1/2 lb.)	227 g
9 oz.	255 g
10 oz.	283 g
11 oz.	312 g
12 oz. (3/4 lb.)	340 g
13 oz.	369 g
14 oz.	397 g
15 oz.	426 g
16 oz. (1 lb.)	454 g
24 oz. (1 1/2 lb.)	582 g
32 oz. (2 lb.)	907 g
36 oz. (2 1/2 lb.)	1 kg
48 oz. (3 lb.)	1.4 kg
64 oz. (4 lb.)	1.8 kg
52 oz. (4 1/2 lb.)	2 kg

Oven Temperature Conversions		
Fahrenheit	**Centigrade**	**Description**
225 F	105 C	Very Cool
250 F	120 C	
275 F	130 C	Cool
300 F	150 C	
325 F	165 C	Moderately Cool
350 F	180 C	Moderate
375 F	190 C	
400 F	200 C	Moderately Hot
425 F	220 C	Hot
450 F	230 C	
475 F	245 C	Very Hot

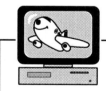

An excellent website for international recipes:

► http://belgourmet.com/sitegb/index.html

Itinerary: You Snooze You Lose

1. Picture the ultimate dream bedroom, just for you. Brainstorm a list of all of the things you would need and want in your dream bedroom. Determine the size of the room, the wall and floor coverings, the furniture, and the gadgets that will be placed in the room.

2. Make a rough sketch of your plan before putting it on graph paper. Remember to think about where you would put doors, windows, and closets.

3. Use graph paper and the scale of $\frac{1}{2}$ inch equals one foot to make a scale drawing of your room. Make sure that you also draw your furniture to scale. Measure the dimensions of some real-life objects or look up their measurements for guidelines. (Example: A twin-size bed is approximately $3\frac{1}{2}$ feet wide and $6\frac{1}{2}$ feet long. So, you would draw it $1\frac{3}{4}$ inches wide and $3\frac{1}{4}$ inches long.)

4. Next, construct a scale model of your plan. You model's scale will be one-square inch equals one-square foot. Use cardboard box scraps (cut to size) for your scale model.

5. Now select the type of wall covering, floor covering, furniture, and gadgets you would like to have in your room. Use the cost sheet on Boarding Pass EH-M5 to figure out how much money this room will cost your parents.

Departure Date: _____ **ETA:** _____

Mileage Perks: *Up to ★★4,000 Frequent-Flyer Miles★★*

Destination Skills: *research, problem solving, creative and critical thinking*

Boarding During: *Mathematics or Art*

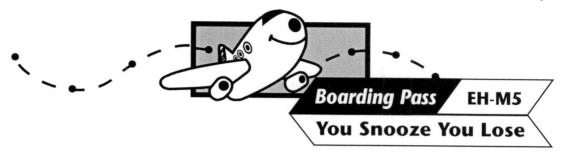

Boarding Pass | **EH-M5**

You Snooze You Lose

Cost Sheet

Floor Covering: Carpeting is sold by the square yard. Once you have calculated the square footage of your room, change this number into square yards. Call or visit a local carpet shop to review what type of carpeting you would like to have in your room, then figure the cost. Make sure you ask about padding and installation. Also calculate the sales tax.

Carpeting $ _____
Padding $ _____
Installation $ _____
Sales tax $ _____
Total $ _____

Wallcovering: Wallpaper is sold in single or double rolls. Rolls vary greatly in price and size. You will have to know how many square feet or square yards of wall space you will cover to arrive at the proper quantity. Stores that sell wallpaper have charts to help you calculate this.

A website that will assist you with your calculations and allow you to view various wallpaper patterns is:
► www.villagehome.com

Paint: Paint is sold by the gallon. First, determine how many square feet of wall space a gallon of paint covers, then determine how many square feet of wall space you need to paint.

Wallpaper per roll (or double roll) x number of rolls $ _____
Paint per gallon x number of gallons $ _____
Sales tax: $ _____
Total $ _____

Furniture and Gadgets: Next, decide on furniture and electronic devices. Use catalogs, newspaper or magazine advertisements, or the Internet to determine the cost of the furniture, computer, televisions, and so on. Itemize your furniture expenses below.

_____   _____   _____

_____   _____   _____

_____   _____   _____

What is the total cost of your Dream Room? $ _____

Ticket for Success

Flight # EH-M6

Itinerary: Flex a Hexa

Flexagons were discovered in 1939 by Arthur H. Stone. By simply folding a strip of paper, he made a discovery that caught his attention. A flexagon is a strip of paper folded up, which you can "flex" to reveal different hidden faces. There are many types of flexagons; for example, there is a tri-hexa-flexagon, tetra-tetra-flexagon, hexa-hexa-flexagon, and dodeca-hexa-flexagon.

1. To make a hexa-hexa-flexagon, follow the instructions on Boarding Pass EH-M6. Make a hexa-hexa-flexagon and one of the other types of flexagons. Once you start flexing, you will want to find a way to reveal all of the hidden sides.

2. Investigate how flexagons work. There are several interesting sites about flexagons on the Internet. Use a search engine and search for *flexagons*. Write a one-page instruction sheet explaining how to design a flexagon and how to flex a flexagon, then present it to your classmates. You'll soon have everyone flexing!

3. Make a kaleidoscope from your flexagon by coloring each face with a different pattern.

4. Hexa-hexa-flexagons make interesting greeting cards and promotional materials. Send a hexa-hexa-flexagon greeting to someone who needs his or her spirits brightened. Don't forget to include instructions on how to flex it.

Departure Date: _____ **ETA:** _____

Mileage Perks: *Up to ★★4,000 Frequent-Flyer Miles★★*

Destination Skills: *research, problem solving, creative thinking*

Boarding During: *Mathematics or Art*

Boarding Pass / **EH-M6**

Flex a Hexa

Directions for Constructing a Hexa-Hexa-Flexagon

Materials Needed

▶ approximately three feet of adding machine tape
▶ clear tape
▶ scissors
▶ pencil and/or crayons

Procedure

1. Fold the adding machine tape into 19 equilateral triangles. Make sure you fold back and forth in both directions along the edges of the triangles and make the folds straight and sharp.

Cut Here →  ← Cut Here

2. With the strip of triangles opened out as below, label each triangle consecutively with 1, 2, and 3. (Repeat so that you have six sets of 1, 2, 3. The last triangle will be blank.)

3. Flip the tape over. Label the triangles in pairs, with the numbers 4, 5, and 6 as shown below, leaving the first triangle blank (4, 4, 5, 5, 6, 6, 4, 4, 5, 5, 6, 6, 4, 4, 5, 5, 6, 6).

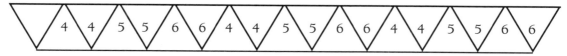

4. Now, starting on the left side, fold the triangles into a spiral, placing 4 on 4, then 5 on 5, then 6 on 6, until the entire tape looks like a squished paper-towel roll.

5. Turn the spiral to the side that has the following pattern showing: 1, 2, 2, 3, 3, 1, 1, 2, 2, 3. Your numbers will appear slanted on the adding machine tape.

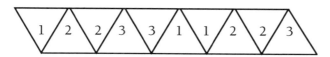

Boarding Pass / **EH-M6**

Flex a Hexa

6. Next, fold the first 2 (the one on the left) *up* to the second 2, and the last 2 (the one on the right) *down* to the next 2.

7. You should see a shape that looks like the one below with the following pattern: blank on top, 3, 3, 3, 1, 1, 1, blank on the bottom.

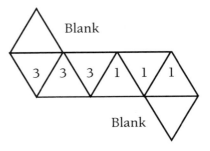

8. Put the 1s in your right hand and the 3s in your left hand and fold in the middle, moving the 3s to the back and keeping the 1s in the front to make a hexagon.

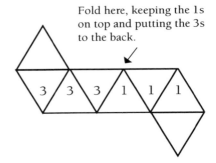

9. Finally, place the blank on top of the blank and tape or glue the blank sides together. You now have a *hexa-hexa-flexagon!* Design the triangles with any patterns you wish, as it will look like a kaleidoscope as you flex it.

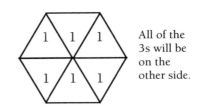

10. **Flexing a hexa-hexa-flexagon.** At position A, put the thumb of your left hand on triangle "a" and the middle finger of your left hand on triangle "b." At position B, put the thumb of your right hand on triangle "d" and the middle finger of your right hand on triangle "c." Pinch these triangles together, and with your index fingers, open the flexagon in the middle like a magic flower. You should have new faces showing. The hexa-hexa-flexagon has six different faces. See if you can find them all!

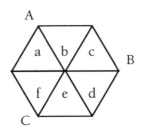

Passport to Learn © 2001 Zephyr Press, Tucson, Arizona • 800-232-2187 • www.zephyrpress.com

Ticket for Success

Flight # EH-M7

Itinerary: The Lucky Seven?

1. Investigate how stocks and the stock market work. See a continuation of Boarding Pass EH-M7 for a website and a few stock abbreviations.

2. Write a three- to five-page report about the stock market. Include definitions and examples of the stock market terms found on a continuation of Boarding Pass EH-M7.

3. Choose seven different stocks to track for the next month. Make sure you choose a good variety (in the stock business, that's called *diversifying your portfolio*). Check the financial pages of a daily newspaper to find the information to complete the chart on Boarding Pass EH-M7.

4. Much of the day-to-day fluctuation in stock prices is a result of human psychology and emotions. The news of the day may affect market prices. Check the front page of a daily newspaper and record the important news of the day on the "Top News Story" chart on Boarding Pass EH-M7. During the month, what news do you think caused the stock market to rise? What news caused a decline in market prices?

5. Make a graph or a series of graphs to show how your seven stocks did during the month.

6. Are you interested in investing in the stock market? Which stocks would you choose now with your newfound financial expertise? Write a reflective paragraph.

Departure Date: _____ **ETA:** _____

Mileage Perks: *Up to ★★4,000 Frequent-Flyer Miles★★*

Destination Skills: *critical thinking, inquiry, research*

Boarding During: *Mathematics or Social Studies*

Boarding Pass / **EH-M7**

The Lucky Seven?

	1		2		3		4		5		6		7	
	Last	Change	Last	Change	Last	Change	Last	Change	Last	Change	Last	Change	Last	Change
1														
2														
3														
4														
5														
6														
7														
8														
9														
10														
11														
12														
13														
14														
15														
16														
17														
18														
19														
20														

Boarding Pass **EH-M7**

The Lucky Seven?

Stock Terms

AMEX	bull market	NASDAQ	Securities and Exchange
asked	capital	NYSE	Commission
averages	commission	OTC	shareholders
bear market	common stock	portfolio	shares
bid	corporation	preferred stock	stock
blue chip	dividends	prospectus	stockbroker
bonds	Dow Jones industrial average	Russell 2000	stock market
brokerage firm	investors	S & P 500	trade

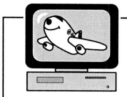

A website that will help you find these terms is:
► http://www.howstuffworks.com/stock.htm
To find the ticker symbol for any stock, go to the following website:
► http://quote.money.com/money/quote/qc

At the ticker symbol website listed above, type any part of the name of a company you know and it will find possible matches. For example, if you want to find the ticker symbol for Toys R Us, just type in "toys" and the site will take you to a list of all possible stocks with *toys* in the company name. At this point, you will be able to locate the company you are looking for and find its ticker symbol. Example: the Toys R Us sticker symbol is TOY. Now, just click on TOY, and it will take you to the current market price for Toys R Us.

Below are listed the 30 stocks in the Dow Jones Industrial Average. The ticker symbol is given for each of these companies. Check the website shown above to find the current market price for some of these stocks.

Ticker	Company Name	Ticker	Company Name
AA	Alcoa	JNJ	Johnson & Johnson
ALD	Allied Signal	JPM	JP Morgan Bank
AXP	American Express	KO	Coca-Cola, Co.
BA	Boeing	MCD	McDonalds
CAT	Caterpillar	MSFT	Microsoft
C	CitiGroup	MMM	Minnesota Mining and Manufacturing (3M)
DIS	Disney	MO	Philip Morris
DD	Du Pont	MRK	Merck
EK	Eastman Kodak	PG	Procter and Gamble
GE	General Electric	SBC	SBC Communications
GM	General Motors	T	AT&T
HWP	Hewlett-Packard	UTX	United Technologies
HD	Home Depot	WMT	Wal-Mart Stores
INTC	Intel	XON	Exxon Mobil
IBM	International Business Machines		
IP	International Paper		

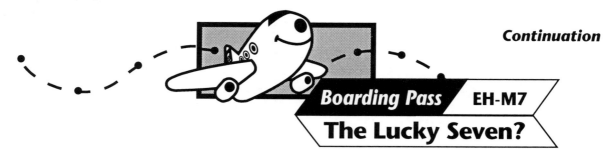

Boarding Pass / **EH-M7**

The Lucky Seven?

Keep track of the news for 20 days.

Date	Top News Story

Passport to Learn ©2001 Zephyr Press, Tucson, Arizona • 800-232-2187 • www.zephyrpress.com

Ticket for Success

Flight # EH-M8

Itinerary: Two Be or Not Two Be

1. Learn about binary numbers (base-2 numbers) by studying Boarding Pass EH-M8.

2. Do some research about the binary system. Why is it important? Use a search engine such as Google or Altavista and search using keywords: *binary numbers* or *binary system*. The first 10 websites listed should give you a great deal of information.

3. Learn how magic squares work by reading the continuation of Boarding Pass EH-M8. Using the magic squares on the continuation of Boarding Pass EH-M8, play the *Magic Square Guessing Game* with your classmates.

4. Be able to explain to your classmates why this trick works by helping them understand the binary or base-2 number system. Use the computer to make charts and visuals to show them how base-2 works.

5. Share this information in a creative way with your class.

Departure Date: _____ **ETA:** _____

Mileage Perks: *Up to ★2,000 Frequent-Flyer Miles★*

Destination Skills: *creative thinking, inquiry, problem solving, research*

Boarding During: *Mathematics*

Boarding Pass | **EH-M8**

Two Be or Not Two Be

The Base-2 System

You are accustomed to using the decimal number system, which contains 10 digits. It is used to count as you are used to counting. However, mathematicians can create any sort of number system they like. For instance, a binary system uses only two digits (0, 1) to form all of the same values that you are used to seeing. See the chart below for an explanation. We can also call this system *the base-2 system* because it is based on only two digits (a base-3 system would be made up of 0, 1, 2; a base-4 system, you guessed it, would use the four digits 0, 1, 2, 3, and so on).

Binary numerals are constructed in the same manner as decimal numerals, with two exceptions:

1. Decimal system: uses 10 digits (0, 1, 2, 3, 4, 5, 6, 7, 8, 9); binary system: uses only two digits (0, 1)

2. Decimal system: each successive place value is 10 times the previous value; binary system: each successive place value is two times the previous value. For example, in the decimal system, 1s place, 10s place 100s place, 1000s place, and so on. In the binary system, 1s place, 2s place, 4s place, 8s place, 16s place, and so on.

Counting in Base 2 (Binary)

	Decimal		Binary	
Value	Number	In words	Number	In words
1	1	one	1	one
2	2	two	10	one-zero (not ten)
3	3	three	11	one-one (not eleven)
4	4	four	100	one-zero-zero (not one hundred)
5	5	five	101	one-zero-one (not one hundred one)
6	6	six	110	one-one-zero (not one hundred ten)
7	7	seven	111	one-one-one (not one hundred eleven)
8	8	eight	1000	one-zero-zero-zero (not one thousand)
9	9	nine	1001	one-zero-zero-one (not one thousand one)
10	10	ten	1010	one-zero-one-zero (one one thousand ten)

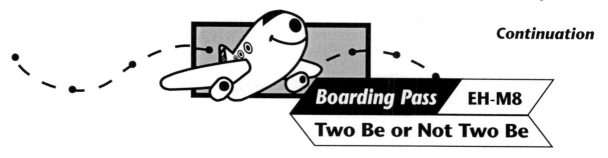

Boarding Pass / **EH-M8**

Two Be or Not Two Be

The chart below explains the two exceptions; remember that binary has only two digits, 0 and 1. Think of "zero" meaning "off" and "one" meaning "on."

Decimal Number	8s place	4s place	2s place	1s place	Binary Number	
1				1	1	(1) = 1
2			1	0	10	(2+0=2)
3			1	1	11	(2+1=3)
4		1	0	0	100	(4+0+0=4)
5		1	0	1	101	(4+0+1=5)
6		1	1	0	110	(4+2+0=6)
7		1	1	1	111	(4+2+1=7)
8	1	0	0	0	1000	(8+0+0+0=8)
9	1	0	0	1	1001	(8+0+0+1=9)
10	1	0	1	0	1010	(8+0+2+0=10)

Another way to explain:

The decimal number 15 is expressed as 1 ten and 5 ones, or 15.

In binary 15 is expressed as 1 eight, 1 four, 1 two, and 1 one, or 1111: 8 + 4 + 2 + 1 = 15.

Boarding Pass / **EH-M8**

Two Be or Not Two Be

Magic Square Directions

Show a friend the six cards that are on the continuation of this boarding pass (facing page). Tell your friend to think of any number from 1 through 63. Ask the following:

Is your number on Card A? Your friend answers "yes" or "no."
Is your number on Card B? Your friend answers "yes" or "no."
Is your number on Card C? Your friend answers "yes" or "no."
Is your number on Card D? Your friend answers "yes" or "no."
Is your number on Card E? Your friend answers "yes" or "no."
Is your number on Card F? Your friend answers "yes" or "no."

You can immediately tell him or her what number he or she has chosen. While your friend is answering "yes" or "no," you add in your head the *first* numbers of the cards on which your friend answered "yes." For example, say your friend chooses the number 37.

Is your number on Card A? Yes. (In your head, add 1.)
Is your number on Card B? No.
Is your number on Card C? Yes. (In your head, add 4.)
Is your number on Card D? No.
Is your number on Card E? No.
Is your number on Card F? Yes. (In your head, add 32.)

$$1 + 4 + 32 = 37$$

How It Works

- The Magic Square cards work on the principle of the binary system. It helps to understand this by remembering that 1 = "on" and 0 = "off."
- The first number on the card represents the first six place values of the binary system: 1, 2, 4, 8, 16, 32.
- If a number appears on the card, that *place value* will have to be turned "on."

Example: To express the number 43 in binary, you would have to turn "on" the 1, 2, 8, 32 places, because $1 + 2 + 8 + 32 = 43$.

As you see, you will only find 43 on the cards that are needed. Simply add the first number on each of those cards in you head. Your friends will think you know math magic, so have fun!

Boarding Pass EH-M8

Two Be or Not Two Be

Magic Squares

A

1	15	29	43	57
3	17	31	45	59
5	19	33	47	61
7	21	35	49	63
9	23	37	51	
11	25	39	53	
13	27	41	55	

B

2	15	30	43	58
3	18	31	46	59
6	19	34	47	62
7	22	35	50	63
10	23	38	51	
11	26	39	54	
14	27	42	55	

C

4	15	30	45	60
5	20	31	46	61
6	21	36	47	62
7	22	37	52	63
12	23	38	53	
13	28	39	54	
14	29	44	55	

D

8	15	30	45	60
9	24	31	46	61
10	25	40	47	62
11	26	41	56	63
12	27	42	57	
13	28	43	58	
14	29	44	59	

E

16	23	30	53	60
17	24	31	54	61
18	25	48	55	62
19	26	49	56	63
20	27	50	57	
21	28	51	58	
22	29	52	59	

F

32	39	46	53	60
33	40	47	54	61
34	41	48	55	62
35	42	49	56	63
36	43	50	57	
37	44	51	58	
38	45	52	59	

Boarding Pass / **EH-M8**

Two Be or Not Two Be

Changing a Number from Base 10 to Another Base

1. Draw a horizontal line on your paper.

    Example: _____

2. Draw a vertical line near the right end of the horizontal line.

    Example: _____

3. Write a base 10 number on top of the horizontal line and to the right of the vertical line.

    Example: _____ 73

4. Write *base* ___ on the bottom of the horizontal line and to the right of the vertical line.

    Example: _____ 73
                                                           BASE_____

5. Decide what base you will change the base-10 number to and write that number next to the word *base*.

    Example: _____ 73
                                                           BASE TWO

6. Divide the base-10 number by the new base number and record the answer on top of the horizontal line and the remainder on the bottom of the horizontal line (in this case, divide 73 by 2).

    Example: _____ 36 | 73
                                                             1 | BASE TWO

Passport to Learn © 2001 Zephyr Press, Tucson, Arizona • 800-232-2187 • www.zephyrpress.com

Boarding Pass / **EH-M8**

Two Be or Not Two Be

7. Draw another vertical line.

Example: _____

	36	73
	1	BASE TWO

8. Repeat steps 6 and 7 until the number on top of the horizontal line is zero.

0	1	2	4	9	18	36	73
1	0	0	1	0	0	1	BASE TWO
64s place	32s place	16s place	8s place	4s place	2s place	1s place	

9. The number written below the horizontal line is the base-10 number, now written in the new base.
   Example:
   1001001 (in base two) = 73 (in base 10)
   1001001 (in base two) = 64 + 8 + 1 = 73 (in base 10)

10. Now try changing 73 into other bases, such as base 5, base 8, or base 12.

Use a search engine and keywords: **binary numbers**
   ▶ www.google.com or www.altavista.com
This is a good website:
   ▶ http://telecom.tbi.net/history1.html#ascii

Ticket for Success

Flight # EH-M9

Itinerary: Crack the Code

Secret codes that adults can't understand are always fun and interesting. Knowing what you know about counting in number systems other than the decimal system, you can generate secret codes that only you and your friends and the cleverest of mathematicians can crack!

1. Investigate ASCII (American Standard Code for Information Interchange) on Boarding Pass EH-M9. ASCII is based on the binary number system, or base 2.

2. Write a secret note to a friend using the ASCII code. See the sample on the continuation of Boarding Pass EH-M9. Be sure to give your friend a key to your code.

3. Create other number system codes, such as octal and hexadecimal codes. Write your message using these codes. See the continuation of Boarding Pass EH-M9.

4. Study and report on other codes. Start by researching the Morse code and the Nato Phonetic Alphabet found on Boarding Pass EH-M9. Find out about Braille, sign language, or semaphores as other forms of codes. Write a two- to three-page report on one of these codes.

5. Extension: Perhaps you can think of a way to make an ASCII code board work as an electric board (see Boarding Pass EH-SC8) or use magnets to either repel (for zero) and attract (for one).

Departure Date: _____ **ETA:** _____

Mileage Perks: *Up to ★2,000 Frequent-Flyer Miles★*

Destination Skills: *research, critical thinking, and problem solving,*

Boarding During: *Mathematics or Language Arts*

Passport to Learn ©2001 Zephyr Press, Tucson, Arizona • 800-232-2187 • www.zephyrpress.com

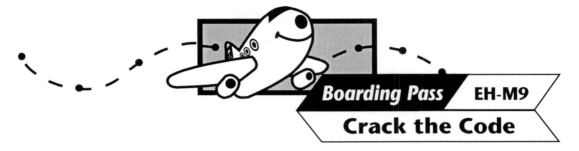

Boarding Pass / **EH-M9**

Crack the Code

To create ASCII code, the inventor first had to come up with a different decimal number to represent every possible lower-case letter, upper-case letter, punctuation symbol, and even spaces and computer commands like *enter* or *delete*. Then the decimal number had to be converted into binary code of 1s and 0s so that the computer could read them. This meant changing every decimal number into a seven-digit binary number. If we wanted to, we could create new codes based on ASCII, by changing from a binary number or decimal number to a hexadecimal number or octal number or any other number system you can dream up. This Boarding Pass shows only the ASCII codes for the upper-case letters and a few special characters (., ?, and space).

CHARACTER	DECIMAL	ASCII or BINARY	HEXA-DECIMAL	OCTAL
A	065	1000001	41	101
B	066	1000010	42	102
C	067	1000011	43	103
D	068	1000100	44	104
E	069	1000101	45	105
F	070	1000110	46	106
G	071	1000111	47	107
H	072	1001000	48	110
I	073	1001001	49	111
J	074	1001010	4A	112
K	075	1001011	4B	113
L	076	1001100	4C	114
M	077	1001101	4D	115
N	078	1001110	4E	116
O	079	1001111	4F	117
P	080	1010000	50	120
Q	081	1010001	51	121
R	082	1010010	52	122
S	083	1010011	53	123
T	084	1010100	54	124
U	085	1010101	55	125
V	086	1010110	56	126
W	087	1010111	57	127
X	088	1011000	58	130
Y	089	1011001	59	131
Z	090	1011010	5A	132
SPACE	032	0100000	20	040
.	046	0101110	2E	056
?	063	0111111	3F	077

To find the ASCII characters for lowercase letters, numbers, and additional symbols, use keyword: **ASCII** or check the following website:
► http://telecom.tbi.net/ascii7s/html/html.

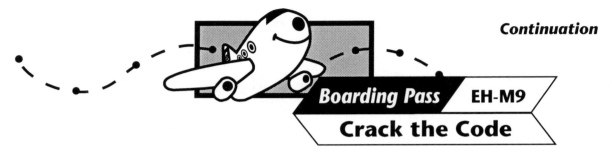

Boarding Pass / **EH-M9**

Crack the Code

Octal

Octal numerals are constructed in the same manner as decimal numerals, with two exceptions:

1. The decimal system has 10 digits (0, 1, 2, 3, 4, 5, 6, 7, 8, 9). The octal system has eight digits (0, 1, 2, 3, 4, 5, 6, 7).

2. In the decimal system, each successive place value is 10 times the previous value. In the octal system, each successive place value is eight times the previous value.
    Example: Decimal system—1s place, 10s place 100s place, 1000s place, and so on
    Octal system—1s place, 8s place, 64s place, 512s place, and so on

Counting to 20 in the octal system is shown below:

Decimal	Octal	Decimal	Octal
1	1	11	13 (pronounced one-three)
2	2	12	14 (pronounced one-four)
3	3	13	15 (pronounced one-five)
4	4	14	16 (pronounced one-six)
5	5	15	17 (pronounced one-seven)
6	6	16	20 (pronounced two-zero)
7	7	17	21 (pronounced two-one)
8	10 (pronounced one-zero)	18	22 (pronounced two-two)
9	11 (pronounced one-one)	19	23 (pronounced two-three)
10	12 (pronounced one-two)	20	24 (pronounced two-four)

Another way to explain:

The decimal number 15 is expressed as 1 ten and 5 ones, or 15.

In octal, 15 is expressed as 1 eight and 7 ones, or 17: 8 + 7 = 15

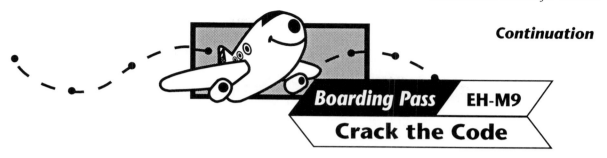

Boarding Pass / **EH-M9**

Crack the Code

Hexadecimal

Hexadecimal numerals are constructed in the same manner as decimal numerals, with the same two exceptions:

1. The decimal system has 10 digits (0, 1, 2, 3, 4, 5, 6, 7, 8, 9); the hexadecimal system has 16 digits (0, 1, 2, 3, 4, 5, 6, 7, 8, 9, A, B, C, D, E, F)

2. In the decimal system, each successive place value is 10 times the previous value. In the hexadecimal system, each successive place value is 16 times the previous value.
   Example: Decimal system—1s place, 10s place 100s place, 1000s place, and so on
   Octal system—1s place, 16s place, 256s place, 4096s place, and so on.

Counting to 32 in the hexadecimal system is shown below:

Decimal	Hexadecimal	Decimal	Octal
1	1	16	10 (pronounced one-zero)
2	2	17	11 (pronounced one-one)
3	3	18	12 (pronounced one-two)
4	4	19	13 (pronounced one-three)
5	5	20	14 (pronounced one-four)
6	6	21	15 (pronounced one-five)
7	7	22	16 (pronounced one-six)
8	8	23	17 (pronounced one-seven)
9	9	23	18 (pronounced one-eight)
10	A	25	19 (pronounced one-nine)
11	B	26	1A (pronounced one-A)
12	C	27	1B (pronounced one-B)
13	D	28	1C (pronounced one-C)
14	E	29	1D (pronounced one-D)
15	F	30	1E (pronounced one-E)
		31	1F (pronounced one-F)
		32	20 (pronounced two-zero)

Another way to explain:

The decimal number 27 is expressed as 2 tens and 7 ones, or 27.

In hexadecimal, 27 is expressed as 1 sixteen and B ones, or 1B: 16 + 11 = 27

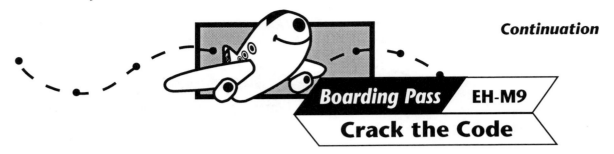

Boarding Pass / **EH-M9**

Crack the Code

ASCII Code Sample

Read the chart below from top to bottom and from left to right, using the ASCII code:

○	= Zero
●	= One

H	=	1001000
E	=	1000101
L	=	1001100
L	=	1001100
O	=	1001111

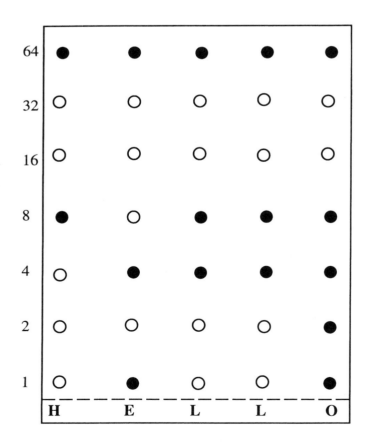

Passport to Learn © 2001 Zephyr Press, Tucson, Arizona • 800-232-2187 • www.zephyrpress.com

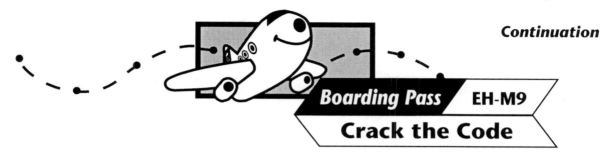

Boarding Pass / **EH-M9**
Crack the Code

Other Code Systems

The Morse Code is a system of dots, dashes, and spaces used by telegraph operators and amateur radio operators to send messages. The Morse Code is named for Samuel F. B. Morse who was largely responsible for the invention of the telegraph. The code consists of different combinations of dots, indicated by the sound of a short tone, and dashes, indicated by the sound of a long tone three times longer than a dot. These are also referred to as *dit* and *dah*. The space between letters is equal to three dots.

Morse Code			
A .-		**N** -.	
B -...		**O** ---	
C -.-.		**P** .--.	
D -..		**Q** --.-	
E .		**R** .-.	
F ..-.		**S** ...	
G --.		**T** -	
H		**U** ..-	
I ..		**V** ...-	
J .---		**W** .--	
K -.-		**X** -..-	
L .-..		**Y** -.--	
M --		**Z** --..	

Nato Phonetic Alphabet

A system of words identifying the letters of the alphabet. The system was reached through international agreement, and uses words chosen for their ease of pronunciation by people of all language backgrounds. Pilots use this alphabet in their radio messages.

A	ALPHA	N	NOVEMBER
B	BRAVO	O	OSCAR
C	CHARLIE	P	PAPA
D	DELTA	Q	QUEBEC
E	ECHO	R	ROMEO
F	FOXTROT	S	SIERRA
G	GOLF	T	TANGO
H	HOTEL	U	UNIFORM
I	INDIA	V	VICTOR
J	JULIET	W	WHISKEY
K	KILO	X	X-RAY
L	LIMA	Y	YANKEE
M	MIKE	Z	ZULU

Ticket for Success

Flight # EH-M10

*Itinerary: Playing the Bases

Some mathematicians have argued that the most practical base for a numbering system is 12 rather than 10. For years, many people have maintained that base 10 is not the best choice for a calculating system. Base 12, also known as "duodecimal" or by the more modern term, "dozenal," has often been mentioned by mathematicians as a possible replacement for base 10. After all, there are 12 hours in the day and 12 in the night. Our year has 12 months and we often buy eggs, baked goods, and other items by the dozen.

1. Using your favorite search engines, investigate the advantages of using base 12 and construct support for changing our number system to a dozenal system.

2. Come up with at least a dozen reasons for why base 12 is better than base 10. Present your findings in a creative manner. Use the *Product Ideas* list (page 42) to assist you in coming up with the best way to present your findings to a group of mathematicians.

* There is no Boarding Pass for this ticket.

Departure Date: _____ **ETA:** _____

Mileage Perks: *Up to ★2,000 Frequent-Flyer Miles★*

Destination Skills: *research, critical thinking, and problem solving*

Boarding During: *Mathematics or Language Arts*

Chapter 9

Expanding Horizons
Tickets for Success

Science

Ticket for Success

Flight # EH-SC1

Itinerary: 20/20 Vision for the Future

You are a scientist in the year 2020. The world population has grown to more than 8 billion people—over 2 billion more people than in 2000. Continued advances in agricultural and medical technology have significantly lowered the death rate while the birthrate remains high. You have been hired to help save the Earth (its plants, animals, humans, and environmental conditions).

1. Use the Creative Problem-Solving process to solve at least one of the problems that overpopulation is causing for the Earth. The five steps in the *Creative Problem-Solving process are:

   - Fact finding
   - Problem finding
   - Idea finding
   - Solution finding
   - Acceptance finding

   The Creative Problem-Solving guide on Boarding Pass EH-SC1 will assist you in solving an environmental problem for the citizens of Earth.

2. Creatively present your solution to your class or an environmental group in your community.

*Permission to reprint the five-stage Osborn/Parnes Creative Problem-Solving process granted by The Creative Education Foundation.

Departure Date: _____ **ETA:** _____

Mileage Perks: *Up to ★2,000 Frequent-Flyer Miles★*

Destination Skills: *problem solving, creative thinking*

Boarding During: *Science or Language Arts*

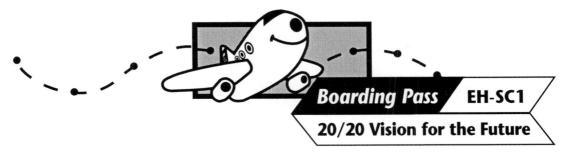

Boarding Pass / **EH-SC1**

20/20 Vision for the Future

The Mess

By 2020, overpopulation in some areas of the world has caused great stress on Earth's resources. The Earth has a limited capacity to renew itself and to safely absorb wastes. Demand for resources continues to grow. More energy is needed, adding to pollution, wastes, and global-warming problems. More land is required for agriculture, housing, factories, and roads, leading to deforestation, soil erosion, and water pollution. You are a concerned scientist of our world. How can you help to protect the Earth from these menacing problems?

Use Creative Problem Solving to come up with solutions to Earth's future problems.

Step 1: Fact Finding

Using only the facts from *The Mess,* above, write down some facts. Consider:

Who is involved?

What is happening?

When is it happening?

Why is it happening?

How is it happening?

What other factors should we consider when looking for solutions to the problems caused by the size of the human population and how it is affecting the Earth?

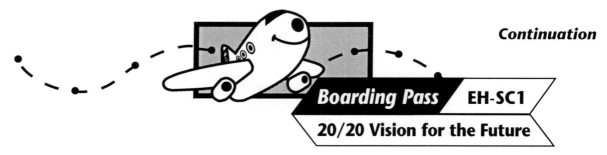

Boarding Pass / **EH-SC1**
20/20 Vision for the Future

Step 2: Problem Finding

Now take these facts and use the facts to generate questions that scientists could brainstorm, research, and solve. Complete the following question: In what ways might a scientist of Earth in 2020 . . . (for example: solve global warming problems?)

1. In what ways might a scientist of Earth in 2020 . . .

_____

_____

_____

2. In what ways might a scientist of Earth in 2020 . . .

_____

_____

_____

3. In what ways might a scientist of Earth in 2020 . . .

_____

_____

_____

4. In what ways might a scientist of Earth in 2020 . . .

_____

_____

_____

5. In what ways might a scientist of Earth in 2020 . . .

_____

_____

_____

- Read over your questions.
- Add or change words.
- Ask yourself why after reading each question.
- Do you need to write another question?
- Pick the question you like best.
- Circle it.

Passport to Learn © 2001 Zephyr Press, Tucson, Arizona • 800-232-2187 • www.zephyrpress.com

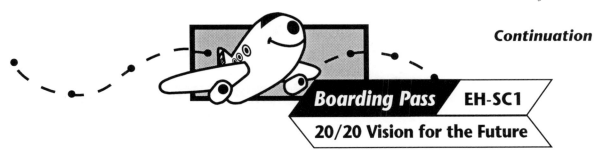

Boarding Pass / **EH-SC1**

20/20 Vision for the Future

Step 3: Idea Finding

Now put your best problem question on the line below and begin thinking of 10 or more ways to solve this problem. You might have a group of friends help you brainstorm some ideas.

In what ways might a scientist of Earth in 2020 _____

Brainstorming Rules

- Don't judge yourself or each other.
- Write down anything that comes to your mind.
- Come up with lots of ideas.
- Group ideas together where possible.
- Think of how you might improve an idea.

My ideas to solve this problem are:

1. _____
2. _____
3. _____
4. _____
5. _____
6. _____
7. _____
8. _____
9. _____
10. _____

Draw one of your ideas below:

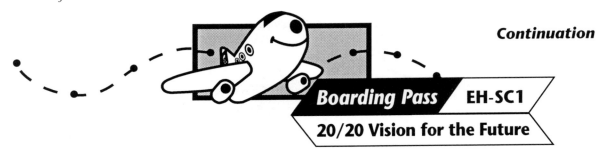

Boarding Pass / **EH-SC1** /
20/20 Vision for the Future \

Step 4: Solution Finding

Go back to Idea Finding (step 3) and select three ideas you really like. Write out your three favorite ideas under *Ideas* in the chart below. (A sample chart that is already completed for a different problem is shown on the next page of this Boarding Pass.)

Ideas	Criterion	Criterion	Criterion	Criterion	Tally
1.					
2					
3.					

Now you must judge, compare, or choose between the ideas. Choose four criteria from the list on Boarding Pass SC1 (continuation 6) or think of your own criterion to put in each grid in the criterion boxes.

Judge your ideas by each criterion. Give three points to the best choice, two points for the next best, and one point to a maybe. Write these numbers in the boxes on the grid. Add them across for each idea. Put the total in the tally boxes.

Which idea has the highest score?

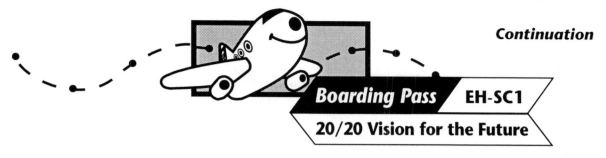

Boarding Pass / **EH-SC1**

20/20 Vision for the Future

Example

Imagine your problem was: How do we preserve and protect wetlands? The best solutions are listed under Ideas in the chart below. The criteria that I used to make the decision are listed across the top of the chart. Each idea was judged according to the criteria and a rating was assigned to each idea:

3 = best, 2 = next best, 1 = maybe.

Ratings for each idea were added together and total points were put in the Tally column.

How do we preserve and protect wetlands?

Ideas	Criterion	Criterion	Criterion	Criterion	Tally
	will help the most people	will protect the most plants and animals	will have the longest lasting effects	will have the most immediate effects	
1. Create city ordinances that prevent development on or near wetlands.	1	3	3	3	10
2 Manage storm water by recreating wetlands.	2	2	2	1	7
3. Increase public appreciation and understanding of wetland function.	3	1	1	2	7

Conclusion: My best idea for preserving and protecting wetlands is to create city ordinances that prevent development on or near wetlands.

Boarding Pass / **EH-SC1**
20/20 Vision for the Future

Possible Criteria to Use with the Problem-Solving Model

1. How practical will this be?

2. How safe will this be?

3. How effective will this be?

4. How easily can this be carried out?

5. How inexpensive will this be?

6. How supportive will others be?

7. How widespread will the support be?

8. How challenging will this be?

9. How far reaching will the benefits be?

10. How much attention will this get?

11. How beneficial will this be?

12. How satisfied will I be?

13. How easy will it be to obtain the necessary equipment?

These criteria suggestions were adapted from a 1980s workshop presented by Joyce Juntune in Grand Rapids, Mich.

Passport to Learn © 2001 Zephyr Press, Tucson, Arizona • 800-232-2187 • www.zephyrpress.com

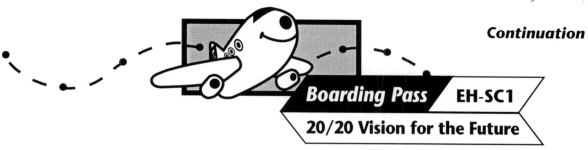

Boarding Pass / **EH-SC1**

20/20 Vision for the Future

Step 5: Acceptance Finding

Write your *best* idea here and make it an acceptable idea.

My best idea is:

Who can help me?

What will help me?

When is the best time?

What is the best way to go about this?

Consider barriers. Watch out for . . .

Be careful of . . .

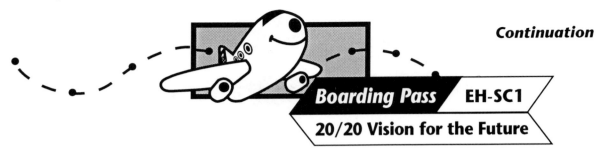

Boarding Pass / **EH-SC1**

20/20 Vision for the Future

Plan of Action

Use your acceptance-finding statements to help develop your plan by completing the statements below.

So, the concerned scientist in 2020 set out to solve the environmental problems of Earth caused by overpopulation.

First,

Then, he or she

Finally, he or she evaluated his or her success and decided

and he or she lived creatively ever after, solving Earth's problems using Creative Problem Solving. Until the next adventure . . . The End.

Ticket for Success

Flight # EH-SC2

Itinerary: Spectacular Sequels

1. Choose something new you want to make or something you want to make better. To get ideas for inventing, try to think of problems, inconveniences, or needs that are currently unmet.

2. Inventing is the creative processes of preparation, incubation, illumination, and verification.

   - *Preparation:* You have a new, exciting, big idea. Now, think what exactly it is that you want to do and write it down, sketch it, and/or make a model of it. Think of some of the problems you might encounter. Review all available information and resources about your idea, including previous unsuccessful attempts to solve the problems and why they did not work.

   - *Incubation:* Set your incomplete ideas aside for a while and do some reflection about your ideas so far.

   - *Illumination:* New ideas suddenly come to you. This is the "Ah-ha" stage of the process, when you will really start to develop your ideas. However, you will probably spend weeks making improvements on your idea or invention.

   - *Verification:* Check to see if your invention works as you thought it would. If it does, investigate how to patent it. If your invention doesn't work out, continue to make improvements until you are satisfied.

Boarding Pass EH-SC2 will give you helpful questions to guide you through the invention process.

Departure Date: _____ **ETA:** _____

Mileage Perks: *Up to ★2,000 Frequent-Flyer Miles★*

Destination Skills: *problem solving, creative thinking*

Boarding During: *Science or Language Arts*

Boarding Pass / EH-SC2
Spectacular Sequels

Ask yourself:

1. What do I want to make, or what do I want to make better?
2. What product or process will this invention provide that does not exist now?
3. How will this invention improve on what exists now?
4. What is the best way to make a rough model, sketch or outline of my invention?
5. How can I improve my invention?
6. Does my invention do what I hoped it would? If not, how can I make it better?

If you think you have come up with an original invention, register a patent with the U.S. Patent and Trademark Office.

If you are stuck, begin by thinking of product or process improvements for the following:

grocery bags	*ice cream*	*Zamboni® machine*	*paper plates*
fruit drinks	*candy bars*	*toothbrushes*	*the school lunch line*

To make these improvements, you might want to use the S.C.A.M.P.E.R. technique to get your thinking started. This technique, developed by Bob Eberle, is used as a checklist to stimulate ideas. S.C.A.M.P.E.R. stands for the following:

S = substitute what?
C = combine what?
A = adapt, make it fit.
M = magnify, minify what?
P = put it to other uses.
E = what else? who else?
R = reverse or rearrange what?

Rube Goldberg (1883–1970) was a Pulitzer Prize-winning cartoonist, sculptor, and author. His drawings of absurdly connected machines that accomplished simple tasks in extremely complex, roundabout means are interesting to study. Check out some of his famous drawings on the website or use keywords: **Rube Goldberg.**

▶ http://www.rube-goldberg.com/gallery.htm

To learn about registering a patent for your invention, visit the United States Patent and Trademark Office website or use keywords: **United States Patent Office.**

▶ http://www.uspto.gov/

Ticket for Success

Flight # EH-SC3

Itinerary: Do It Again: Recycled Science

1. From recycled materials, such as 35mm film canisters, many scientific devices or instruments can be created. Follow the directions on Boarding Pass EH-SC3 to create a kaleidoscope.

2. First, gather the materials listed on Boarding Pass EH-SC3.

3. Following the procedures, construct your kaleidoscope with the help of an adult.

4. Enjoy your kaleidoscope and share it with a friend.

5. Write a brochure with text and graphics to explain the scientific workings and construction of a kaleidoscope.

6. Do an Internet search using keywords: *film canister*. Make a poster explaining at least five additional scientific things you can make using a 35mm film canister (for example: seed-growing containers, string telephone, parachute, and so on).

7. Extension: For a community service project, visit a sick child (or children) in the hospital. Bring this person your kaleidoscope as a gift to brighten her or his day. Explain the science of the kaleidoscope in a way that the child will understand.

Departure Date: _____ **ETA:** _____

Mileage Perks: *Up to ★2,000 Frequent-Flyer Miles★*

Destination Skills: *research, problem solving, creative thinking*

Boarding During: *Science, Reading, or Language Arts*

Boarding Pass / **EH-SC3**

Do It Again: Recycled Science

Film-Canister Kaleidoscope

Materials

- ► 2 black 35mm film canisters
- ► 3 microscope slides or three 1-inch-by-3-inch pieces cut from an overhead transparency sheet or any colorless plastic of similar width
- ► 1 empty Tic-Tac® box
- ► beads or sequins (enough to fill one-half of the empty Tic-Tac® box)
- ► hot-glue gun or masking tape
- ► drill with 1/2-inch wood bit and 1/4-inch wood bit
- ► scissors (if using transparencies)

Procedure

Note: Adults will have to do the drill work and the hot-glue-gun work. If using microscope slides, adults will have to help with this as well.

1. Drill a 1/4-inch hole in the end of one black film canister and drill a 1/2-inch hole in the end of the other.

2. If using a transparency, use the scissors to cut three 1-inch-by-3-inch pieces.

3. While holding the three pieces of glass or plastic in the palm of your hand, form an equilateral triangle. Keeping the triangle formation, carefully insert the pieces of glass or plastic into the open end of one of the film canisters. They will be wedged in place. Place the second film canister over the sticking out pieces of the triangle.

4. Use a hot-glue gun (or masking tape) to seal the joined ends of the film canisters together.

5. Add beads or sequins to an empty Tic-Tac® box. Glue the box on the end of the film canister with the large hole.

6. Observe objects through your kaleidoscope by holding the small hole to your eye.

Scientific Explanation

A kaleidoscope is a long tube containing three mirrors running the length of the tube and set at an angle to each other. You look through a peephole between the mirrors at objects at the other end. If the angle between each of the mirrors is 60, 45, or 30 degrees, you see a series of images reflected in the mirrors.

From a demonstration by Denise McCarthy and Elynn Severson at the National Science Teachers Association Convention in Las Vegas, Nev., 1998.

Ticket for Success

Flight # EH-SC4

Itinerary: Finagle a Bagel

1. Learning about science through food is always fun and interesting. Use a bagel to conduct each of the experiments listed on Boarding Pass EH-SC4 and fill out the chart for each experiment.

2. After conducting the experiments, find out the scientific principles behind a pendulum, probability, buoyancy, simple machines, molds, and so on, by checking various resources, such as websites and reference books.
   - pendulum: study Galileo's laws of the pendulum
   - probability: study the probability shown in Pascal's triangle
   - buoyancy: study Archimedes' principles of buoyancy

   Study definitions and examples of simple machines and molds. Use the terms in the list above to begin your investigation.

3. Write a brief description of each principle.

4. Compare and contrast or analyze the results of your experiments with your findings from investigating these scientists and principles.

5. Conduct a professional conference. Pretend to be a professor and teach your classmates the experiments and the scientific principles behind them.

6. Extension: Develop science experiments using other types of foods; peanuts or popcorn, for example.

Departure Date: _____ **ETA:** _____
Mileage Perks: *Up to ★2,000 Frequent-Flyer Miles★*
Destination Skills: *research, problem solving, creative thinking*
Boarding During: *Science, Reading, or Language Arts*

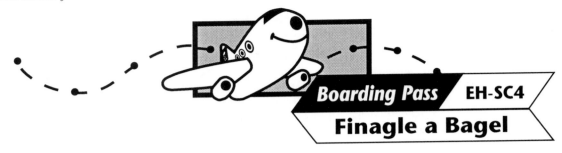

Boarding Pass / EH-SC4

Finagle a Bagel

Finagle-a-Bagel Experiment A: Up Close and Personal

1. Can you pick your bagel out of a crowd?

2. Observation is a scientific processing skill. Work with a group of four to six classmates for this activity. Your teacher will give each of you a bagel, magnifier, paper, pencil, and ruler.

3. Each person receives a bagel. Look closely. What unique characteristics does your bagel have? Note any distinguishing characteristics.

4. As you collect data, perform the following:
   - draw your bagel with its distinctive characteristics
   - measure your bagel
   - weigh your bagel, if scales are available

5. After each person has a chance to observe his or her bagel, place all of the bagels together. Can you find yours among a group? How do you know you are right?

Finagle-a-Bagel Experiment B: Swinging Bagels

1. What determines the number of swings per minute that a bagel will make when suspended from a string?

2. In order to experiment with pendulums as Galileo did many years ago, you will need at least two bagels of different diameters, string, a watch with a second hand, and a ruler or tape measure. Make sure you record all of your findings.

3. Tie a piece of string to a bagel and begin swinging it. However, consider these variables and how you will control them in an experiment:
   - What size of bagel will you use?
   - What length will the string be for each trial?
   - How many combinations of string length and bagel size will be tested?
   - What will you count as one swing?
   - What will the starting swing be?
   - How many trials will each size of bagel receive, and each string length receive?

Finagle-a-Bagel Experiment C: Falling Bagels

1. Is it true that bagels always land cream cheese side down?

2. In order to experiment with probability, you will need bagels, cream cheese, plastic knives, newspapers, a spoon, and a ruler or tape measure. Make sure you record all of your findings.

3. Apply cream cheese to one side of a sliced bagel, then drop the bagel and see which side lands face-up. However, consider these variables and how you will control them in an experiment:
   - How will you cut the bagel?
   - How much cream cheese will you apply? To which side? How will you measure the amount?
   - From what height will you drop the bagel? Will the data be different if the height is varied?
   - How will you hold the bagel—cut side parallel or perpendicular to the floor?
   - How many times will you drop the bagel?

Boarding Pass / **EH-SC4**

Finagle a Bagel

Experiment A: Up Close and Personal

Draw your bagel here. Make sure you include any distinctive characteristics.

What are your bagel's measurements?   Other notes:

Approximate diameter: _____   _____

Approximate height: _____   _____

Weight: _____   _____

_____

_____

_____

Experiment B: Swinging Bagels

Trial Number	Bagel Size (diameter)	Number of Swings in 10 Seconds

Trial Number	String Length	Number of Swings in a Minute

Duplicate these charts on a separate piece of paper for each bagel size and for each string length. Try each bagel size at least seven times. Try each string length at least seven times.

Experiment C: Falling Bagels

Trial Number	Cream Cheese Up	Cream Cheese Down

You might want to try the following additional experiments with bagels:

- Do bagels float? Whole? Half? How long? Does cut side up or cut side down make a difference?

- Cut bagels in such a way as to make interesting prints. Can one group duplicate another group's prints?

- Does a sample group of bagels roll down a given plane for the same distance? Compare bagels of different diameters, and different ramp angles.

- How do various types of bagels (onion, garlic, egg, and so on) serve as a growth medium for molds?

This exercise was adapted with permission from Hands On Science Outreach (HOSO), Silver Springs, Md., which first developed a Bagelmania workshop for a presentation at the National Science Teachers Association Convention in 1988.

Ticket for Success

Flight # EH-SC5

Itinerary: Your Wi$h I$ Granted

The National Science Teachers Association (NSTA), in conjunction with Craftsman, Duracell, and Toshiba, sponsor awards and contests each year that challenge students to use their creativity, imagination, and knowledge of science and technology. A brief description of each contest and information on how to receive entry materials are listed on Boarding Pass EH-SC5.

1. Enter one of these contests by following the guidelines or search for additional science or technology awards, contests, and grants. Additional resources are listed on Boarding Pass EH-SC5.

2. Also look for information that will give you helpful hints on writing grants and applying for contests and awards.

Departure Date: _____ **ETA:** _____

Mileage Perks: *Up to ★2,000 Frequent-Flyer Miles★*

Destination Skills: *research, inquiry, creative and critical thinking*

Boarding During: *Science or Language Arts*

Young Inventors Awards Program

Purpose: The Craftsman/NSTA Young Inventors Awards Program challenges students to use creativity and imagination along with science, technology, and mechanical ability to invent or modify a tool.

Eligibility: The Young Inventors Awards Program is open to all students in grades 2–5 and 6–8 in the United States and U.S. Territories.

To receive entry materials:
Craftsman/NSTA Young Inventors Awards Program
National Science Teachers Association
1840 Wilson Blvd.
Arlington, VA 22201-3000
1-888-494-4994
younginventors@nsta.org

Duracell/NSTA Invention Challenge

Purpose: The Duracell/NSTA Invention Challenge invites students to design and build a device which runs on Duracell® batteries; entrants write a two-page description of the device and its uses, submit a wiring diagram of the device, and a photograph of the device.

Eligibility: The Duracell/NSTA Challenge is open to students in grades 6–9 and 10–12.

To receive entry materials:
Duracell/NATA Invention Challenge
1840 Wilson Blvd.
Arlington, VA 22201-3000
1-888-255-4242

Toshiba/NSTA ExploraVision Awards

Purpose: ExploraVision students work in groups of two, three, or four, along with a team coach. They first select a technology that is present in the home, school, and/or community. Next, they explore what the technology does; how it works; how, and when, and why it was invented. Students must then project what that technology could be like 20 years from now. Finally, they submit a written description and five graphics simulating web pages.

Eligibility: Primary level (K–3), upper elementary level (4–6), middle level (7–9)

To receive entry materials:
Toshiba/NSTA ExploraVision Awards
1840 Wilson Blvd.
Arlington, VA 22201-3000
1-800-EXLORE-9
www.toshiba.com/tai/exploravision/

Ticket for Success

Flight # EH-SC6

Itinerary: Destination: Your Own Creation

1. The Space Exploration Initiative has set a goal to establish a permanent colony on the surface of Mars. You are a U.S. space program scientist who has been assigned to the Mars Colony Design Team. Your mission is to list and draw floor plans for the key areas of a Mars colony, which are shown on Boarding Pass EH-SC6. Remember that gravity on Mars is about one-third of that on Earth.

2. Before you begin planning, decide why a Mars colony should be created. Ask yourself the following questions: Are you there to mine Martian minerals? Are you there to study scientific phenomena in a nearly weightless environment? Are you studying stellar events? Are you planning to develop sites for Earth's waste and garbage? Is a Mars colony being established as a gateway to the solar system?

3. Once you have established the mission, goal, or theme, decide on a name for your soon-to-be-established Mars colony.

4. Plan your colony: draw a blueprint with graphic and descriptive text. See Boarding Pass EH-SC6 for several important components that should be considered in order to create a successful colony.

5. Design a logo for the colony that will be used for patches and flags.

6. Create a slogan that will capture the theme of your mission.

Departure Date: _____ **ETA:** _____
Mileage Perks: *Up to ★★★6,000 Frequent-Flyer Miles★★★*
Destination Skills: *creative and critical thinking, higher-level thinking*
Boarding During: *Science, Art, or Language Arts*

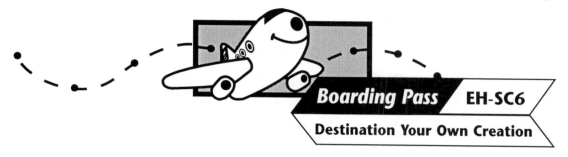

Boarding Pass / **EH-SC6**

Destination Your Own Creation

Draw plans for the following important areas and describe where these areas will fit into the entire plan for your Mars colony.

Medical Site

- Consider emergency needs, surgical areas, dental areas, isolation areas, and so on.
- Draw a floor plan and label each area.
- List your equipment needs.

Communications Site

- Think about how the people on your Mars colony will communicate . . .
  1. between the Earth and Mars
  2. between one another while on Mars
- Draw a floor plan of the communications area.

Transportation Site

- Design the vehicles that the Mars colonists will use to get around for short-, medium-, and long-range traveling.
- Draw a floor plan of the transportation area, including the repair and vehicle storage areas.

Housing Site

- Design your eating area, including preparation, serving, and storage facilities.
- Consider how you will grow some of your own food on the Mars colony.
- Design the inside of your dining facility, making sure you have created a pleasant atmosphere for Mars colonists.

Recreational Site

- Design a recreational facility where your Mars inhabitants will relax and have some fun.
- Consider types of exercise machines and gymnasiums you will have, adjusting for the lower gravity on Mars.
- Design additional amusements, especially games that would be fun to play in lower gravity.

Power Site

- Design the facility that will supply power for the entire Mars colony.
- Think of how you will control emissions.

Waste-Management Site

- Design equipment and facilities that will manage garbage and human waste.
- Think of recycling options.

Security Site

- Design safety and crime-fighting equipment and facilities.

Itinerary: Put the Story to the Test

Early elementary teachers must spend a great deal of time in their classrooms teaching reading and language arts.

1. Help an early elementary teacher in your school by providing him or her with suggestions for at least three different pieces of literature that could be followed up with science activities or experiments. Focus especially on physical science topics such as electricity, magnetism, air, balance, light and color, density, gravity, heat, mixtures, sound, states of matter, and so on.

2. Begin by searching your school library for books that could have a science connection.

3. Next, search for resources (books and websites) that contain physical science experiments.

4. Write lessons plans for the teacher, including materials and procedures to carry out your experiments. See the sample lesson on Boarding Pass EH-SC7, which could be used after reading a book such as *Mirette on the Highwire,* by Emily Arnold McCully which introduces students to the concept of balance.

Departure Date: _____ **ETA:** _____

Mileage Perks: *Up to ★2,000 Frequent-Flyer Miles ★*

Destination Skills: *creative and critical thinking, research, inquiry*

Boarding During: *Science or Reading*

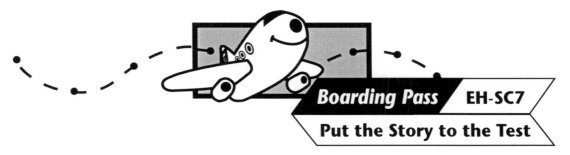

Boarding Pass / EH-SC7

Put the Story to the Test

What to include in a lesson plan for elementary teachers:

1. The title of the book: _____

2. The science concept in the book: _____

3. What do students need to learn about the science concept?

4. What knowledge do students need to know in order to understand the science concept?
   List any important terms and definitions.

5. What activity/experiment could students perform to help them understand the science concept?

6. What materials will you need for this activity or experiment?

7. What steps will the students need to do to complete the activity or experiment?
   Use steps of the scientific method to design your activity or experiment.

   • What observation will the students make?

   • What question will the students investigate?

   • What predictions might the students make?

   • What procedures will the students use to test their predictions?

   • How will the students record the results of their investigation?

   • What conclusions might the students draw after completing the investigation?

Ticket for Success

Flight # EH-SC8

Itinerary: **Spark of Genius**

1. Research and study at least four current topics in science that you would like to know more about. The following list will help you get started:

aeronautics	chemistry	quantum physics
animals	dinosaurs	plants
archaeology	earthquakes	the scientific method
bacteria	genetic engineering	string theory
black holes	the human body	the solar system
the brain	natural disasters	weather

2. Teach others about scientific topics by developing a series of electric boards for at least four topics listed here.

   - Make an electric board of the skeletal system: Draw a skeleton and list the bones of the body on your electric board. Then connect the name of each bone to the correct picture of that bone on your drawing of the skeleton.
   - Make an electric board of the Periodic Table. Match the names of the elements to their symbols.

   Directions for making an electric board are shown on Boarding Pass EH-SC8.

Departure Date: _____ **ETA:** _____

Mileage Perks: *Up to ★2,000 Frequent-Flyer Miles ★*

Destination Skills: *creative and critical thinking, research, inquiry*

Boarding During: *Science*

Passport to Learn © 2001 Zephyr Press, Tucson, Arizona • 800-232-2187 • www.zephyrpress.com

Making an Electric Board

- Cut two 9-inch-by-12-inch pieces of posterboard or oak tag, or use a manila folder.
- Create two columns. One column will provide terms or questions, the other column gives the answers (as shown below).
- Punch a hole on the outer edge of each column to correspond to each term, question, and answer.
- On the back of the posterboard, connect each term or question to its correct answer with a 1-inch-wide strip of aluminum foil, folded to a ¼-inch width. *Important*: before adding a new piece of aluminum foil, cover each strip completely from the back with masking tape.
- Using two-sided tape or glue, fasten the second piece of posterboard to the back of the first, covering up all of your aluminum strips and tape.
- Using a continuity tester, which can be purchased in any hardware department, check every circuit. Touch the question with one end of the tester and its related answer with the other. If there is a match, the bulb on the tester will light up. Now let your friends try!

Parts of an Airplane

● Fuselage	Used to control the pitch of an airplane	●
● Aileron	Part of the trailing edge of the wing; provides control in roll and banking	●
● Elevator	Main structural body of an aircraft	●
● Rudder	Part of the trailing edge of the wing; designed to increase lift	●
● Flaps	Attached to the tail; controls the yaw	●

Do not limit yourself to making columns. You can arrange terms, questions, and answers in any way you see fit. Matching pictures or diagrams with terms or definitions works very well too. Use your creativity to make electric boards that teach others.

Now that you have created your board, hypothesize about why and how it words. Ask your friends for their ideas.

Ticket for Success

Flight # EH-SC9

Itinerary: Cleared for Takeoff

1. Create a paper airplane contest with a series of events for a group of students, such as your classmates, a scout troop, or any other club or organization involving students.

2. Before holding the contest, investigate the parts of a real airplane to discover how airplanes fly. Discover the function of the elevator, rudder, ailerons, and flaps. Use sources to investigate paper airplanes and what makes them aerodynamic. Discover how you can design them to simulate the movements that real planes have to do, such as ascend, descend, and turn. Also, investigate Bernoulli's Principle, so that you understand how air pressure affects the flight of a plane.

3. Make patterns for several different types of paper airplanes and write directions for making each of your planes.

4. Write the rules for your paper airplane contest. Suggestions are given on Boarding Pass EH-SC9.

5. Present the rules to your teacher and/or your principal for approval before holding the contest.

6. Hold your contest. Then write a short paper reflecting on the success of the contest and what you would change if you were to hold another paper airplane contest.

Departure Date: _____ **ETA:** _____
Mileage Perks: *Up to ★2,000 Frequent-Flyer Miles ★*
Destination Skills: *creative and critical thinking, research, inquiry*
Boarding During: *Science and Language Arts*

Boarding Pass / EH-SC9

Cleared for Takeoff

Think of the following when designing your paper airplane contest.

1. What will you name your contest?

2. Design an application for participants who want to enter the contest.
    *   Include the date, time, and place for the contest.
    *   Have participants include information such as name, age, and grade.
    *   Have parents of participants sign the application giving permission to enter the contest.
    *   Include rules for the contest on the application.

3. Make posters advertising the contest.
    *   Include information similar to what is on the application.
    *   Make the posters colorful and easy to read.

4. Decide on a site for your contest.
    *   Draw a diagram for each of the different events you will hold during the contest. Examples for a variety of events:
        a. paper airplane that lands closest to a designated spot
        b. paper airplane that flies the longest distance.
        c. paper airplane that makes a sharp left or right turn
        d. paper airplane that stays in the air for the longest time
        e. paper airplane that climbs at a steep ascent.

5. Determine the materials needed for the contest.
    *   Do you need stopwatches, tape measures, paper and pencil? Other materials?

6. Set rules for the contest. Think about things such as:
    *   How much paper can be used for the planes in the contest? One 8½-inch-by-11-inch sheet?
    *   How many attempts can each contestant make for each different competition?

7. Design a certificate for winners of each event and for different age groups.

Check out the following resource: *Kids' Paper Air Plane Book* by Ken Blackburn and Jeff Lammers.

Itinerary: Thrill Seekers

1. Read about the science of amusement parks as explained on Boarding Pass EH-SC10.

2. Research a famous scientist or inventor. (See Boarding Pass EH-SC10 for ideas.) Apply the scientific theories or discoveries of the scientist you researched to design rides for your own amusement park. The rides can be related in concept, construction, theory, or theme.

3. Explain how your rides relate to the scientific theories or discoveries in a short, one-page description.

4. Sketch plans for your rides, create three-dimensional models, or construct a pop-up book of your creations. An excellent resource is *How to Make Pop-Ups,* by Joan Irvine. The author's website is http://www.makersgallery.com/joanirvine/howto.html

5. Design a brochure to advertise your theme park. Be sure to give it a creative name. Remember that you want to appeal to children and adults.

Departure Date: _____ **ETA:** _____

Mileage Perks: *Up to ★2,000 Frequent-Flyer Miles ★*

Destination Skills: *creative and critical thinking, research, inquiry*

Boarding During: *Science*

Boarding Pass **EH-SC10**

Thrill Seekers

Amusement park rides are based on theories of physics.

Visit the following website to design your own roller coaster and experiment with bumper car collisions. This site is great fun, and you can learn a lot about roller-coaster safety.

> ► www.learner.org/exhibits/parkphysics

Another website that has some great hyperlinks to help you discover how the laws of physics affect amusement park ride design can be found at

> ► http://themeparks.about.com/travel/themeparks/msub24.htm

Think about some famous scientists, inventors, or pioneers in the medical field. Research what they did and use your findings to develop your own theme park. You might want to consider:

- Sir Isaac Newton and his laws of motion
- The Wright Brothers and the first flight
- Elijah McCoy, who helped trains and all things with engines, move more smoothly and safely (have you ever heard of the "Real McCoy?")
- Frances Gabe and her self-cleaning house
- Alexander Graham Bell and the telephone
- Thomas Alva Edison and the light bulb

Perhaps you would like to find out more about Dr. Christian Barnard, a pioneer in the field of heart transplants, and design a human-body theme park with a ride that would take thrill seekers through the human heart.

You can find information about many additional scientists and inventors on the following website:

> ► http://www.inventorsmuseum.com

Bibliography

Agee, Jon. 1999. *Sit on a Potato Pan, Otis!: More Palindromes.* New York: HarperCollins.

———. 1998. *Who Ordered the Jumbo Shrimp? and Other Oxymorons.* New York: HarperCollins.

Blackburn, Ken, and Jeff Lammers. 1996. *Kids' Paper Air Plane Book.* New York: Workman.

Botermans, Jack, and Pieter van Delft. 1978. *Creative Puzzles of the World.* New York: Abrams.

Coil, Carolyn. 1999. *Teaching Tools for the 21st Century.* Dayton, Ohio: Pieces of Learning.

Davis, Gary A., and Sylvia B. Rimm. 1998. *Education of the Gifted and Talented.* Boston, Mass.: Allyn & Bacon.

Eberle, B., and Stanish, B. 1985. *CPS for Kids.* Carthage, Ill.: Good Apple.

Galbraith, Judy. 1983. *The Gifted Kids' Survival Guide (For Ages 11–18).* Minneapolis, Minn.: Free Spirit.

Gertz, Susan E. 1996. *Teaching Physical Science through Children's Literature.* Middletown, Ohio: Terrific Science Press.

Henage, Diana. 1990. *The Gifted Intervention Manual.* Columbia, Mo.: Hawthorne Educational Services.

Irvine, Joan. Illustrated by Barbara Reid. 1987. *How to Make Pop-Ups.* Toronto: Kids Can Press.

Juntune, Joyce. 1982. *Creative Problem Solving for the Classroom Teacher.* San Ramon, Calif.: One Hundred Twenty Creations.

Kaufeldt, Martha. 1999. *Begin with the Brain: Orchestrating the Learner-Centered Classroom.* Tucson, Ariz.: Zephyr Press.

Kovalik, Susan, and Karen Olsen. 1992. *Integrated Thematic Instruction: The Model.* Kent, Wash.: Books for Educators.

Lewis, Barbara. 1991. *The Kid's Guide to Social Action: How to Solve the Social Problems You Choose and Turn Creative Thinking into Positive Action.* Minneapolis, Minn.: Free Spirit.

————. 1998. *What Do You Stand For?* Minneapolis, Minn.: Free Spirit.

Lipson, Greta B. 1998. *Poetry Writing Handbook.* Carthage, Ill.: Teaching and Learning.

Lipson, Greta B., and Bernice N. Greenberg. 1981. *Extra! Extra! Read All About It.* Carthage, Ill.: Good Apple.

Marzano, Robert J., and Debra J. Pickering. 1997. *Dimensions of Learning Teacher's Manual.* Alexandria, Va.: ASCD.

McCully, Emily A. 1992. *Mirette on the High Wire.* New York: Putnam and Grosset.

Parke, Beverly. 1989. *Gifted Students in Regular Classrooms.* Boston, Mass.: Allyn and Bacon.

Piirto, Jane. 1998. *Understanding Those Who Create.* Scottsdale, Ariz.: Gifted Psychology Press.

Sisk, Dorothy, and Hilda Rosselli. 1987. *Leadership: A Special Kind of Giftedness.* Monroe, N.Y.: Trillium Press.

Slovacek, Cindy. 1996. *Open for Business.* San Luis Obispo, Calif.: Dandy Lion.

Treffinger, D. J., Isaksen, S. G., and Dorval, K. B. 1994. *Creative Problem Solving: An Introduction* (revised). Sarasota, Fla.: Center for Creative Learning.

Tunnell, Lorrie. 2000. *Flight.* Westminster, Calif.: Teacher Created Materials.

Winebrenner, Susan. 1992. *Teaching Gifted Kids in the Regular Classroom.* Minneapolis, Minn.: Free Spirit.

The World Almanac and Book of Facts. 2001. Mahwah, N.J.: World Almanac Books.

About the Author

Jacque Melin was a teacher and coordinator of gifted and talented students for over 20 years and served as an elementary principal for five years. She is currently a visiting professor at Grand Valley State University, where she works with student teachers and teaches classes in gifted and talented education. *Passport to Learn* is Jacque's first book.

Zephyr Press

From the Publisher

With a philosophy that learning should be significant and fun, I founded Zephyr Press in 1979. Many on our staff are former educators. We are all committed to quality education and, in addition to our work, volunteer with schools and young people.

We know that the teachers, parents, and staff developers who use our products are looking for tools that are practical, easy to use, and incorporate the best and latest in educational research. We are proud that our customers have come to trust us. They know how careful we are to ensure that the products we sell meet high standards.

You'll note that most of our titles emphasize the kind of teaching that uses the multiple intelligences theory and brain-compatible learning environment and are appropriate for high-potential learners. Many of the activities within our products integrate disciplines so that the learning is more meaningful and significant. Our products are the best because our authors are top-notch. They are among the brightest educators around, and it's an honor to publish their work.

If you enjoy browsing the Internet, be sure to visit our online catalog at www.zephyrpress.com.

Joey Tanner

Joey Tanner, M.Ed.
Founder and President

Your Students Are Ready. Are You?

Engage them with these resources to promote active learning

IMAGITRONICS
Mind-Stretching Scenarios to Launch Creative Thought and Develop Problem-Solving Skills
Don Ambrose, Ph.D.

While traveling, you see a strange game being played in a stadium. Three teams of eight players each are chasing an oversized rubber ball on a large triangular field . . . How is this game played? What are the rules? Draw several players in action.

Don Ambrose's delightful *Imagitronics* gives you and your students 71 unique and inventive scenarios to stimulate creative and critical thinking and artistic design. In the example above, your students will imagine how this peculiar sport is played and may even set up a practice field to try it out. These fantastic scenarios and quirky illustrations will enrich the minds of the brightest children and engage the interest of those who are currently underachieving.

Grades 4–10
160 pages
ISBN: 1-56976-141-8
1171-W . . . $29.95

CYBERTRIPS IN SOCIAL STUDIES
Online Field Trips for All Ages
Scott Mandel, Ph.D.

Cybertrips in Social Studies takes you and your students on virtual field trips to faraway people, long-ago places, and to the heart of incidents that shaped our world, its history, and its cultures.

The interactive nature of the World Wide Web allows you and your students to *be there*—whether "there" is in an igloo at the Arctic circle or at Place de la Bastille in 18th-century France. The 12 complete trips include community, history, and humanities field trips such as Jobs People Have, Families and Cultures, Ancient Greece, Democracy, and The Homeless.

Grades K–12
144 pages
ISBN: 1-56976-145-0
1170-W . . . $26.95

INVENTING TOYS
Kids Having Fun Learning Science
Ed Sobey, Ph.D.

Capture your students' full attention and excitement. Transform learning science and math concepts into a creative, stimulating discovery adventure. *Inventing Toys* makes it easy to teach through brilliant, tried-and-true creative problem-solving experiences and to tie inventing adventures to your science curriculum. You'll get—

- Directions for 6 inventing workshops including toy boats, toy cars, pneumatic-blast rockets, and more
- Toy Inventor's Log Journal and Report sheets
- Thorough step-by-step instructions, materials lists, and room layout suggestions
- National Science Education Standards and American Association for the Advancement of Science Benchmarks

Grades 4–8
ISBN: 1-56976-124-8
144 pages
1121-W . . .$23.00

More Favorites from Zephyr Press

ART MATTERS
Strategies, Ideas, and Activities to Strengthen Learning across the Curriculum
Eileen S. Prince, M.A.

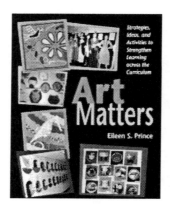

Are you a history or math teacher looking to improve your curriculum? Perhaps the art program at your school has been cut and you've been asked to add art to your teaching schedule, or maybe you're the administrator who knows that students who study the arts do better on such tests as the SAT. These easy-to-use strategies and lesson plans will help both classroom and art teachers integrate art across the curriculum.

Grades K–12
192 pages
ISBN: 1-56976-129-9
1152-W . . . $27.95

Best Seller
KIDVID
Second Edition
Fun-damentals of Video Instruction
Kaye Black, M.Ed., NBCT

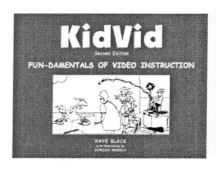

Even if you have never held a video camera, this classroom-tested resource can help you give your students a valuable start in video production. This comprehensive guide now includes guidelines and rubrics for assessing videos and content, tips on how to create special effects, and more skill-building activities.

Help your students learn the basics of video production, develop analytical skills, construct criteria for evaluating video production, and utilize creative thinking and problem-solving skills while they demonstrate their knowledge.

Grades 4–12
112 pages
ISBN: 1-56976-104-3
1013-W . . . $22.95

Order Today!

Qty.	Item #	Title	Unit Price	Total

Name _____

Address _____

City _____

State _____ Zip _____

Phone (_____) _____

E-mail _____

Method of payment (check one):

❑ Check or Money Order   ❑ Visa

❑ MasterCard   ❑ Purchase Order Attached

Credit Card No. _____

Expires _____

Signature _____

Subtotal	
Sales Tax (AZ residents, 5.6%)	
S & H (10% of subtotal–min $5.50)	
Total (U.S. funds only)	

CANADA: add 30% for S & H and G.S.T.

Please include your phone number in case we have questions about your order.

Call, write, e-mail or Fax for your FREE Catalog!

Zephyr Press

P.O. Box 66006-W
Tucson, AZ 85728-6006

1-800-232-2187
520-322-5090
Fax 520-323-9402
neways2learn@zephyrpress.com

— Order these resources and more any time, day or night, online at **www.zephyrpress.com** or **www.i-home-school.com** —